MW01194355

Month of the Sacred Heart

Month of the Sacred Heart

or

PRACTICAL MEDITATIONS FOR EACH DAY
OF THE MONTH OF JUNE

by the

ABBÉ BERLIOUX

Translated from the Sixth French Edition by
LÆTITIA SELWYN OLIVER

WITH PREFACE BY THE

REV. R. J. CARBERY, S.J

MEDIATRIX PRESS
MMXXII

ISBN: 978-1-957066-28-8

𝕹𝖎𝖍𝖎𝖑 𝖔𝖇𝖘𝖙𝖆𝖙
P. J. TYNAN, S.T.D.
Censor Theol. Depot.

𝕴𝖒𝖕𝖗𝖎𝖒𝖆𝖙𝖚𝖗:
✠ GULIELMUS J. CANON Walsh
Vic. Cap. Dublinensis.
Dublini,
Die 20 mens. Maii 1885.

© Mediatrix Press, 2022.
Month of the Sacred Heart was originally published in 1884 by Gill and Sons, as a translation of *Mois du Sacré-Coeur : méditations pratiques pour chaque jour*, published in 1875.
The Mediatrix Press edition has been reprinted in conformity with the original. All the typography and layout of this edition are copyrights of Mediatrix Press, all rights reserved. No part of this edition may be reproduced in print or electronic format without the express permission of the publisher. No part of this work may be placed on archive.org.

Cover art: *Sagrado Corazón de Jesús*
—Eduardo Tresguerras, 18th - 19th century

607 E 6th Ave.
Post Falls, ID 83843
www.mediatrixpress.com

Table of Contents

PREFACE

THIS little work is of the kind most useful in the present stage of devotion to the Sacred Heart. Until very recently the important point was to bring home to the faithful that, even as in the old dispensation, when some great sorrow was crushing down the people of God, He was wont to cheer them by a message from on high, so now, in these days of danger for souls, His compassion has been moved to reveal to us a special preservative against the incredulity and selfishness of the age. This great fact is at present well proclaimed. There are few Catholics who have not heard of the wondrous mission confided to Blessed Margaret Mary, and who have not, at some time or other, been moved to ponder over its import for their souls. *"The voice of the Beloved has been heard in the land. Behold I stand at the gate and knock: if any man will open to me I will come in to him and sup with him."*

The work, therefore, which now presents itself to all who would cooperate in our Blessed Lord's design, is to open hearts to receive the devotion in its plenitude, that the divine promises may be fulfilled. It is essentially a devotion of the heart. Its special power is to soften the heart in the spirit of love, and thus to aid the development of its natural aspirations for what is pure and holy. Now simple, loving, prayerful thoughts are the key to the human heart, and it is only through them that this devotion can enter there. If blessings have been promised to the homes where representations of the Sacred Heart are exposed and honored, it is because such representations are calculated to excite such thoughts of the Redeemer's love. With the growth of Confraternities in our days, and the increased spiritual instruction of their members, what can be more efficacious for this end than the diffusion of simple, suggestive manuals of meditation, conceived in the spirit of the devotion? This last condition is most important, and should be secured by all who wish to practice and propagate the devotion, *as it was instituted by our Divine Lord.* The character of works purporting to treat of the Sacred Heart, which are occasionally published in France and elsewhere, proves the need of more widely diffused light on the primary principles of the devotion. Those principles have been most accurately defined by saints and theologians; and yet, at times, pious authors are content with the vaguest conceptions of the devotion, overlooking the fundamental fact that, though it is in one sense *universal,* because its object, being divine love, must necessarily be the center around which other devotions move, yet it is, above all, a *most special* devotion, with a character so peculiarly its own, that without it, it ceases to be the devotion to which the divine promises are attached.

This work, which appears now for the first time in English, is the outcome of a theological intelligence of the devotion, perfected in prayer. It is, in reality as in name, a manual of practical meditation for the month of June. Each meditation is suggested by some one of the emblems of divine love disclosed to Blessed Margaret Mary, or by the dispositions of the adorable Heart; its affections, its sympathies, its sufferings, its yearnings for our love. Some simple thoughts on such touching subjects lead to a practical conclusion, strengthened by an appropriate example. In addition to the recommendations of several French bishops, the author has had the honor of receiving a special letter of approval from the late Holy Father. He is the author also of a similar manual for the Month of May, which was published last year by Messrs. Gill & Son.[1]

---

[1] 1884. The *Month of Mary*, along with the *Month of St. Joseph*, is also available from Mediatrix Press.

Amongst the motives for consecrating that sweet month to the Queen of Heaven there was one in the designs of Providence not manifest at first. The Church places on Mary's lips the inspired words: "He who shall find me, shall find life, and draw salvation from the Lord." Now that the Sacred Heart has claimed the month of June for its special honor, it is, indeed, a fitting function for Mary's month to so prepare the hearts of her children, that they may "draw waters in joy from the fountains of the Savior," Isaiah, 12:3.

The Abbé Berlioux's manuals are well calculated to promote this blessed result, and the translator has a claim on the gratitude of English-speaking Catholics for the admirable manner in which she has presented to them such helps to their devotion.

R. J C

Month of the
Sacred Heart of Jesus

FIRST DAY

INVITATION TO SANCTIFY THE MONTH OF THE SACRED HEART

THE devotions of the *Month of Mary* have just been brought to a close, and the result of those devotions should be the resolution to begin well and to sanctify as far as possible the *Month dedicated to the Sacred Heart*. You owe it to that tender Mother, who says to you: "My child, I am the road which leads to Jesus; go, kneel at His holy altar, and there contemplate the beauties and riches of His Divine Heart. I will impart to you My spirit to understand It, my heart wherewith to love It, and each day I will implore It to bless you and to shower down on you the treasures of Its love." The Church unites her voice to that of the Blessed Virgin. The Month of flowers, consecrated to the Queen of heaven, is no sooner ended than she ardently desires, that the month of fruits should be dedicated to the Heart of Jesus; she wills that we should turn from the powerful mediation of our advocate to the infinite mercy of our Savior. The Church says to us with the prophet: "*You shall draw waters with joy out of the Savior's fountains*" Isa. 12:3. The illustrious Pius IX, of holy memory, enriched the Month of the Sacred Heart with many precious indulgences, and uttered the following most consoling words: "*There is no hope for the Church and society but in the Sacred Heart of Jesus; It alone can remedy the evils of these days.*" Finally, Jesus invites and urges us to hasten to His Heart. To each of us He shows His wounded side, as He did to the apostle St. Thomas, saying: "Come, touch, see, and taste the sweetness of my Heart; It belongs to you, and Its delights are to be with the children of men. Come, then, to me during these thirty days consecrated to my honor. Come whatever may be your sorrow and your miseries, and I will refresh you. If you knew the gift of God, if you knew who I am, and what I am able to bestow on you, with what eagerness would you not respond to my loving call."

Let us, then, go, Christians, where the Savior's love summons us; that place, we know well, should be at His feet, like Magdalen, to bedew them with our penitential tears; but since He offers us the privilege of St. John, let us raise ourselves up to that divine and tender Heart:

Month of the Sacred Heart

Accedet homo ad cor altum. "Man shall come to a deep heart." Psal. 63:7. We shall inhale Its fragrance, listen to Its soft voice, make known to It our sorrows, and we shall obtain for ourselves and relations, for the Church, for our beloved country, for the just, and for poor sinners, all we need. We shall be able to say with Solomon, speaking of the gift of wisdom: "Now all good things came to me together with it." Wis. 7:11. That we may spend this month in a proper manner, let us consider, in the presence of God, what are the graces that we hope to gain by our practices of devotion, and let us offer up our prayers, communions, and good works for this intention. Let us have in our rooms a picture of the Sacred Heart: the sight of it will remind us of our practices of devotions, and enkindle in our breasts the fire of divine love. Our Lord has promised that wherever the representation of His Sacred Heart is exposed and venerated, it will be a source of abundant benedictions. We should communicate, if possible, every Friday, and during the day repeat often the invocation: "O Heart of Jesus, burning with love for us, inflame our hearts with Thy love!"

EXAMPLE

A person, known for his devotion to the Heart of Jesus, related the following circumstance: "My grandfather, when eighty years of age, fell dangerously ill. Unfortunately he was an atheist, who believed neither in the existence of God nor the immortality of the soul; he had never had the happiness of making his first Communion. I endeavored to speak to him of the necessity and beauty of the Catholic religion, and more especially of the future state of the soul; but all my arguments were useless. I then had recourse to other means. The month of June was about to begin; I resolved to sanctify it, and to invoke daily the Sacred Heart of Jesus for the conversion of this poor sinner.

My supplications were not in vain; the first day of this blessed month, the merciful Heart of Jesus granted my request; for that evening the parish priest was seen by the bedside of the sick man, instructing him in the principal mysteries of religion. The next day, my grandfather made his confession and received absolution, after which he affectionately thanked the priest, saying: 'Oh, how happy you have made me!'

The day fixed for his first Communion was the fourth of June; he was then to receive that

God so long unknown, who had waited for him with so much patience and goodness. Children, grandchildren, and great grandchildren surrounded his bed, forming, truly, a touching sight. He afterwards sat up, embraced us all, and, warmly pressing each to his heart, wept with joy and happiness. This was not the only favor granted by the Heart of Jesus; for grace was given him to expiate, by much suffering, a life of sin, and this soul, the object of Its predilection, passed from life on the last day of the month dedicated to this adorable Heart." How true it is, O Christians, that we can obtain all we desire during this month of graces, if we invoke the Heart of Jesus with fervor and perseverance.

PRAYER

O good Master and Savior Jesus Christ vouchsafe to accept our loving adoration on this first day of the month dedicated to Thy divine Heart. What Joy to come each day and offer Thee our homage, and what a source of grace and blessings will it be to us. Oh! help us to profit by this holy time; and do thou, O Virgin Mary, our Mother, lead us to the Heart of Jesus, and lend us thine own, with which to love Him. Amen.

SECOND DAY

ORIGIN OF THE DEVOTION TO THE SACRED HEART

THE devotion to the Sacred Heart may be considered as ancient as the Church itself. It began on Calvary, when this divine Heart, transfixed by the lance, opened to all the faithful an assured refuge, and an inexhaustible fountain of grace. For many ages, however, this devotion was practiced only by a few chosen souls, and it was not till the seventeenth century that the Heart of Jesus was honored in a solemn and public manner, France being not only the birthplace, but the center of the devotion. In a monastery of the Visitation, at Paray-le-Monial, in the diocese of Autun, there lived a holy religious whose name in the world had been Margaret Alacoque, but in religion was called Sister Margaret Mary. Her entire life was spent in the closest union with God, and in return He bestowed upon her His choicest graces. One day, during the Octave of the Feast of Corpus

Christi, in the year 1675, Jesus Christ appeared to her, and showing to her His Heart, which bore the mark of that deep and precious wound inflicted on Calvary: "*Behold*," He said, "*the Heart which loves men so ardently, and is so little loved in return!*" He then desired that a special feast should be set apart to honor His Heart, and to offer It a worship of love and reparation; and He promised the most signal blessings to all those who should adopt and spread this devotion. Sister Margaret Mary put forth all her zeal and charity in order to win hearts to the Heart of Jesus. Her generous efforts were crowned with the greatest success; after a short interval of time, the Church authorized the office and Feast of the Sacred Heart, and encouraged all the faithful to take advantage of the inestimable treasures which God, in His infinite mercy, had vouchsafed to offer them. The voice of the Church was heard; the fire of divine love spread from soul to soul, parishes and dioceses caught the holy flame, and at the present time the devotion to the Sacred Heart has revived throughout the world feelings of faith, and piety and love.

In recalling to our minds, O Christians, the origin and propagation of this devotion, let us admire the ingenuity and tenderness of the Sacred Heart of Jesus; let us bless Him for bestowing upon us His favors, and let us ask of Him the grace to profit by them. Oh! if we only knew the gift of God, and how to appreciate the value of the offering He makes us! Let us also cultivate a great devotion to the humble religious to whom Jesus imparted His gracious designs, and who was called by Him the beloved disciple of His Heart. Let us extol this noble daughter of St. Francis of Sales, who became the glory and patroness of France, and was beatified by Pius IX on the 17th January, 1864. Let us beg of her to obtain for us the grace to love the Heart of Jesus as she loved It.

EXAMPLE

During the month of May, 1722, the plague broke out in the town of Marseilles. Death, the king of terrors, erected his mournful throne in the midst of that great city, once so brilliant and so gay. Deserted by all the inhabitants who had it in their power to fly, Marseilles soon became like a battle field, strewn with the dying and the dead. The afflicted town, devastated by the scourge of pestilence, saw her streets and public places encumbered by its victims, priests and doctors decimated by the dreadful visitation, and forty thousand persons, consigned to the grave. Heart-rending shrieks were heard on every side, and the complete annihilation of the ancient city seemed at hand.

It was then that the holy Bishop of Marseilles Monsiguor Belzunce, a model of charity and pastoral zeal, was interiorly enlightened by Almighty God, and inspired with the idea of having recourse to the Sacred Heart of Jesus, of consecrating to It the unfortunate town and diocese, and of establishing in Its honor a solemn and public procession in perpetuity. The magistrates and inhabitants joined in the vow of the venerable prelate, which already gave promise of a speedy deliverance. Marseilles was consecrated to the Sacred Heart, and the procession took place with every demonstration of religious pomp. Suddenly the plague ceased; fear vanished, and the inhabitants returned, and during six weeks not a single death, or sickness of any sort, was known in the town.

"Oh! you whose lives are spent on the waters of the ocean," said the bishop, addressing the sailors of Marseilles, "publish to all nations, even the most uncivilized, the glory, power, and infinite mercy of the Sacred Heart of Jesus, which has worked such wonders in our behalf, and has turned our sorrows into joy."

PRAYER

O Jesus! how wonderful art Thou in the outpourings of Thy love! We bless Thee for communicating to us the treasures of Thy Heart, and ask Thee to grant us Thy divine assistance, that we may profit by them. O Blessed Margaret Mary! friend and apostle of the Heart of Jesus, we congratulate thee that the divine Master selected thee as the instrument to accomplish His merciful designs; obtain for us that this adorable Heart may be always the object of our love, and the pledge of our salvation. Amen.

THIRD DAY

THE PROMISES OF THE HEART OF JESUS

WHEN our Lord manifested to Blessed Margaret Mary His Sacred Heart, He made numerous and most consoling promises to all those souls who should devote themselves to the worship of this adorable Heart. Let us listen to the words of her who received from Jesus Himself the glorious name of well-beloved disciple of His Heart:

"Would that it were in my power to relate all that I know concerning this devotion to the Heart of Jesus, and to make known to all the world the treasures of grace which my Savior desires to pour forth abundantly on all those who shall practice it!

"First, the faithful shall obtain by means of this touching devotion peace in their families; the graces necessary for their state of life; consolation in all their difficulties, and the blessing of heaven on all their undertakings.

"Secondly, sinners shall find in that Sacred

Heart a fountain and boundless ocean of mercy. Tepid souls shall become fervent, and fervent souls shall rise speedily to great perfection. This devotion alone would reestablish fidelity and regularity in the most relaxed religious communities.

"Thirdly, priests who are animated with a tender love for the divine Heart of Jesus, shall have the power of softening the hardest hearts, and their labors shall be crowned with marvelous success.

"Fourthly, those who propagate this devotion shall have their names written in the Heart of Jesus, and they shall never be effaced.

"Fifthly, all Christians shall find in this divine Heart, a secure refuge during life, and especially at the hour of death. Oh! how sweet will it be to die after having constantly persevered in devotion to the Heart of Him who is to be our Judge.

"Lastly, He will bless every house in which the representation of His Sacred Heart shall be exposed and honored."

Behold, then, O Christians, the promises which Jesus has made to men; a God alone could make them; a God alone can fulfil them. He promises everything: conversion for sinners, advancement in perfection for the just, power in preaching and direction of souls, fervor in communities, peace in families, blessings on temporal affairs, and especial protection at the hour of death. Shall we not be inexcusable if, through our own fault we reap no benefit from so many and such magnificent promises? The experience of more than two hundred years has convinced us of their truth. The sick have invoked the Heart of Jesus, and they have recovered their health; sinners have cast their iniquities into that abyss of mercy, and they have obtained pardon; the sorrowful have found comfort, and wavering souls have drawn from the Sacred Heart strength and victory.

Let us, then, turn on all occasions, for everything we need to this powerful, rich, and bountiful Heart; to this Heart overflowing with mercy and love, which desires nothing so much as to accomplish Its promises.

Let us exclaim with the devout St. Bonaventure: "I will speak to the Heart of my God, and I shall obtain from It all that I can want."

EXAMPLE

A certain man had an only child whom he tenderly loved, and to whom he intended to bequeath a rich inheritance. In order to save his beloved son from a cruel death, the father, one day, risked his own life, was taken by his enemies, treated most inhumanly, and finally put to death. The poor orphan would not be comforted, the light of day became hateful to him, and his only wish was to die also. When anyone tried to console him, he would reply weeping: "O my father! my dear father!"

At last a friend devised a plan to comfort him; he enclosed the heart of the father in a casket, and brought it to him. At the sight of this casket containing the heart of his devoted parent, who had sacrificed his life to save him, the poor orphan heaved a deep sigh, and embracing it passionately, he watered with his tears that heart which had loved him so well. From that moment he became resigned to his hard fate; the possession of his treasure gave him comfort, and till his last moment, he never ceased to preserve it with the greatest veneration and respect.

Jesus, who died for us—Jesus, who for us, gave Himself up to the death of the Cross, has carried His love so far as to give us also His Heart; but He gives us a living Heart, full of graces and riches, ever ready to alleviate our woes and to sympathize with our sorrows. Who, after this, could allow himself to be disheartened, to complain or yield to despair, when he remembers the promises that accompanied this divine gift?

PRAYER

My Savior and Master, Jesus Christ, how shall I sufficiently thank Thee for the countless blessings, which Thou hast promised to those who honor Thy Heart; Thy loving Heart, which is like to an overflowing fountain, the waters of which neither time nor eternity can exhaust. Teach me to love, to venerate, and imitate this bountiful and generous Heart, so that I may profit by Its glorious promises.

FOURTH DAY

THE MATERIAL OBJECT OF THE DEVOTION TO THE SACRED HEART

THE material object of the devotion is the Heart of Jesus Christ. One day, exposing His sacred breast, He said to the Blessed Margaret Mary: *"Behold this Heart which loves men so much!"* This, the material object of our worship, is clearly pointed out by the action of the Savior, and the words which were spoken. It is the Heart of the most holy, the most loving, and perfect of the children of men, formed by the Holy Ghost Himself of the pure blood of a Virgin; the masterpiece of heaven and earth, of nature and grace. But this is not all; It is the Heart of a God, since It has been hypostatically united to the Divinity; consequently It is the sanctuary of all possible perfections and merits, a fathomless abyss of graces and benedictions. It is something even more, It is the heart of a God-Man, that is to say, the most wonderful union of all that is purest and most refined in human affections with divine mercy and goodness.

16

In this Sacred Heart compassion is united to mercy, fraternal affection to paternal love. Oh! the depth of the riches of the mercy of God! *O altitudo divitiarum*!

Can we conceive an object more worthy of our respect and love? If the Church honors with a special homage the instruments of the Passion of our Lord, the thorns which crowned His sacred head, the cross on which He died, the spear which pierced His side, how much more are we bound to honor the adorable Heart of Jesus. Is it not the principle of His life, the source of His sufferings and love? Is it not the fountain of that precious blood which purifies us in the sacraments and refreshes us at the altar? St. Bernardine speaks of It as a furnace of love; St. Peter Damien calls It the universal treasure of wisdom and knowledge; St. Francis of Sales, the fountain of all graces. Here on earth we should esteem ourselves happy, could we, after a long separation from a loved parent, offer again our heart's affection, and have we nothing to offer to the Heart of Jesus, the holiest, the tenderest, and most generous of all Hearts.

Christians, Jesus gives us His Heart, and what does He ask of us in return? He asks us for ours. "My Son," He says, "give me thy heart." Our heart must give itself to some object, for it cannot live without loving. On one side the world claims its affections to make of our poor heart a living hell; on the other, Jesus desires ardently to take possession of it, in order to transform it even during this life into a paradise of delights. To whom then shall we give it? To Thee, O Jesus! God of love! to Thee alone will I give my whole heart without return, without reserve, in life and in death, in time and eternity.

> *Sacred Heart of Jesus, I implore,*
> *That I may love Thee more and more.*

EXAMPLE

Fidelity to the Catholic faith was considered high treason in England during the religious persecution of the fifteenth and sixteenth centuries. The faithful were branded with the name of traitor, and as such they were treated at the public tribunal of justice, as well as under the tortures of their execution. The ordinary punishment was that of hanging on the common gallows, the cord was then severed, and the victim fell to the ground, still breathing. Then the hangman, armed with a sharp knife, approached the culprit, and plunging the blade into his breast, pulled out the quivering heart, and showing it to the assembled crowd, cried out: "Behold the heart of a traitor!" It is related that a priest, about to expire under this atrocious mode of torture, collected all his remaining strength, and whilst the executioner searched for his throbbing heart, gave the following magnificent denial to his words: "No that which thou holdest in thy hand is not the heart of a traitor, but a heart consecrated to God: *Quod manu tenes Deo sacratum est.*" His last breath was an act of divine love.

Would to heaven, O Christians, that when on the day of your death, you feel in your breast the last feeble pulsations of your heart, you may be able to resist the demon's hand and cry: "Begone, Satan, begone; this heart does not belong to you. Neither the world nor the passions have sullied it. My heart has throbbed only for the Heart of Jesus. It belongs to God, and has always been His, and shall be His forever: "Deo sacratum est."

PRAYER

Behold, O Jesus! I give Thee my heart; I place it in Thy hands, and beg of Thee to keep it as a precious trust; preserve it for me as Thou didst that of Thy beloved servant Margaret Mary. If ever I have the misfortune to desire to recall my gift, restore it not to me, but oblige me by an act of Thy mercy, to leave Thee master and possessor of it forever. Amen.

FIFTH DAY

THE SPIRITUAL OBJECT OF DEVOTION TO THE SACRED HEART

We have said in a previous chapter that the sensible and material object of our devotion is the actual Heart of Jesus. There is also a spiritual object, which is the essential part of the worship paid to this divine Heart; this object is the love of Jesus for us. "*Behold,*" said He, "*this Heart which loves men so ardently!*" Observe well these words: "*loves men so ardently!*" Jesus has loved all mankind since He died for all, and there is not one who cannot say: "He loved me, and delivered Himself for me." (Gal. 2:20). But to what extent has He loved us? Who can understand the greatness of His love? Jesus Christ Himself appears unable to express it. Recall to your mind some of His many blessings. Remember the crib at Bethlehem, the cross on Calvary, the Eucharist, that sacrament of love, by means of which Jesus will remain with us till the end of time, hidden under the appearance of

21

a little bread, shut up in the tabernacle as in a narrow prison, forgotten and abandoned by nearly all. Is not this a God who loves us with an infinite love? God, as He is, Could He do more? Truly, He has loved us even to the end; He has loved us to excess, yes, to the utmost excess of love: *Usque in finem dilexit eos.* All these marks of love have emanated from the Heart of Jesus. "Yes, it was His heart," said Blessed Margaret Mary, "that made the crib, the cross, the altar; which formed the Church, and instituted the sacraments. It is from His adorable Heart that we receive life, intelligence, and grace." "O Sacred Heart of my Savior!" exclaimed St. Francis of Sales, "O source of supreme love! Who can sufficiently extol Thee! Who can return Thee love for love?"

Christians, let us correspond to this love of Jesus for us by a like love for Him, and according to the expression of St. Magdalen of Pazzi: "Let us love love." Can anything be more just, more reasonable, and more salutary. "*If any man love not our Lord Jesus Christ let him be anathema!*" (1 Cor. 16:22.) It is the apostle St. Paul who utters these terrible words. Let us, then, love Him who has loved us without bounds; our love should be a consuming fire which devours all earthly affections, and enables us, like the same apostle, to set at defiance the united powers of the world and hell. "Who shall separate us from the love of Christ? shall tribulation? or distress? or famine? or nakedness? or danger? or persecution? or the sword? For I am sure that neither death, nor life, nor height, nor depth, nor any other creature shall be able to separate us from the love of God, which is in Christ Jesus our Lord." (Rom. 8:35, 39). O Jesus! Jesus! I will love Thee forever—yes, forever!

EXAMPLE

The following incident, which took place in Canada, in the year 1872, proves how good and merciful is the Heart of Jesus.

A man, advanced in years, had given up frequenting the sacraments for more than thirty years, and not only was he indifferent as to his religious duties, but he was also animated by a dislike and hatred to priests; on every occasion he sought to speak against them, and to turn into ridicule both themselves and their holy office. For many years his family prayed earnestly for his conversion, but in vain. At length a relative, known for her piety, was inspired with the idea of appealing, as a last resource, to the Sacred Heart of Jesus, to which she had a great devotion.

She hastened to the church, obtained a blest medal of the Sacred Heart, and on her return hid it in the clothes of the poor sinner. Her next thought was to have several novenas made in different convents; and after a time, trusting that the united supplications had prevailed with the merciful Heart of her good Master, she sent for a priest, and contrived a meeting between him and the lost sheep she hoped to restore to the fold. The divine Heart of Jesus does not do things by halves: the triumph of grace was complete and miraculous. The sinner, who for so many years had hated the sight of a priest, eagerly welcomed this one; he made his confession with contrition and faith, and from that time it was almost necessary to restrain his zeal for prayer and works of piety.

A few days after is conversion, a visitor ventured to speak ill of priests in his presence; but the unhappy guest soon perceived that he had mistaken his company, and had to remain silent. The family were overjoyed, and the new convert knew not how to show sufficiently his gratitude to the Heart of Jesus, which had withdrawn him from the brink of hell.

PRAYER

O Heart of Jesus! receive the homage of my heart, which is penetrated with admiration and gratitude at the thought of Thy immense love for man. Grant me the assistance of Thy grace, that loving Thee with the most tender end generous love on earth, I may obtain from Thine infinite goodness the favor of glorifying and loving Thee forever with the angels and saints in heaven. Amen.

SIXTH DAY

THE PRESENT STATE OF THE
DEVOTION TO THE SACRED HEART

"Our Lord gave me to understand," said the Blessed Margaret Mary, "that He desired His Sacred Heart should be known *at the present time* as the mediator between God and man, averting the punishments which our sins have drawn down on us. Oh! how all powerful is this Sacred Heart to appease divine justice provoked by our iniquities, and to obtain mercy for us!" The Sacred Heart is indeed necessary to the Church in this century when, as St. Paul says: "Men shall be lovers of themselves, covetous, haughty, proud, blasphemous, disobedient to parents, ungrateful, wicked, without affection, without peace, unmerciful, lovers of pleasures more than of God." (2 Tim. 3:2).

The whole world is rotten to the core, and to escape destruction the faithful must seek fresh life at the fountain-head by entering into the Heart of the King of Heaven. "The society of our days, exclaimed the illustrious Pius IX, of holy memory, "can be saved by the Sacred Heart alone;" and a learned prelate has pronounced that: "The worship of the "Sacred Heart has been reserved to these latter ages as a pledge of divine love, which desires to manifest itself more abundantly as the end of the world approaches. This devotion is the shield of faith and the food of piety in the midst of the errors and disorders of this century." In corroboration of this, have we not seen a general movement amongst the faithful to practice this providential devotion; only a few years ago a hundred thousand pilgrims, of all ranks, and of every nation, knelt at the tomb of Blessed Margaret Mary, at Paray-le-Monial; the banner of the Sacred Heart has been unfurled on the field of battle by the devout children of the Church; many bishops have consecrated their dioceses to the divine Heart; France made a solemn vow to raise a glorious shrine in Its honor in Paris on the smoldering ruins of Montmartre; finally, the much-loved Pius IX, yielding to the solicitations of the entire Catholic world, ordained that the whole Church should be consecrated to the Sacred Heart of Jesus on the 16th July, 1875, the anniversary of the apparition to Blessed Margaret. What a powerful motive have we not, then, for confidence in this devotion, and let each of us repeat those words that have so often been said: "*the Heart of Jesus will save us!*"

Let us be animated with a like faith, for it is the way of salvation. Would it not be closing our hearts to a universal and Catholic instinct, if we were to take no share in this great devotion? Rather let us unite in offering to the Sacred Heart of Jesus our fervent prayers and good works, and thus hasten the deliverance of the Church, and the conversion of our country.

> *God of mighty power*
> *Take Thy Vicar's part*
> *Oh, save him in this hour*
> *For Jesus' Sacred Heart.*

EXAMPLE

We read a very remarkable incident in the life of St. Gertrude, whose soul was so wonderfully enlightened by Almighty God, and to whom He revealed many sublime truths. On the feast of St. John she was favored with a miraculous vision: the beloved disciple appeared to her as at the Last Supper, leaning on the breast of the Redeemer, and at the same moment it was vouchsafed to her to experience something of the ineffable delights which flowed from the Sacred Heart of Jesus unto that of His Evangelist.

St. Gertrude addressing him, said: "Apostle of love, you who had the inexpressible happiness of reposing on the bosom of Jesus, and listening to the beatings of His Heart, why, in your Gospel, did you not speak of the sentiments and adorable riches of this divine Heart?"

"My daughter," replied St. John, "know that to me was confided the charge of instructing the infant Church concerning the person of the Incarnate Word, in order that she might transmit this fundamental truth to future ages.

But God has reserved for these last times the knowledge of the delights and riches of the Heart of Jesus, so that by this means the world, when becoming old and chilled by the universal indifference of mankind, might be renovated by the fire of divine love."

Christians, we now live in the midst of those unhappy times of which the beloved disciple speaks, Alas! the fire of charity is extinguished in nearly all hearts; but let us take courage, devotion to the Sacred Heart will rekindle it. Then from all hearts will arise that cry which will be reechoed by the whole Catholic world: "*Glory to the Sacred Heart of Jesus!*

PRAYER

O Jesus! our loving and adorable Redeemer, in past ages the treasures of Thy Sacred Heart were but little known; this favor Thou didst reserve to these days, when by a wondrous act of Thy love, it has pleased Thee to make known to men the riches of this divine Heart. We will bless and praise for all eternity this Thine infinite mercy, and beg of Thee the grace to profit by it. Amen.

SEVENTH DAY

THE WOUND OF THE HEART OF JESUS

JESUS had breathed forth His last sigh on the hard wood of the cross, and there only remained on Calvary, Mary, the mother of the Savior, Mary Magdalen, and the apostle St. John. Represent to yourself this little group, and imagine that you stand amongst them. A soldier arrives, he draws near, and gazes on the lifeless body of Jesus. "He is dead," he exclaims, "but I will strike him once more;" and aiming his spear at the right side of the Redeemer, he pierces it, and the sharp point of the lance enters in and opens that divine Heart. As he withdraws the weapon, water and blood gush forth from the wound: "*Exivit sanguis et aqua.*" In the words of St. John: "Immediately there came out blood and water." (John, 19:34). These were the last tears, the last drops of blood from the Sacred Heart: truly a miracle of love, a mystery which contains in itself many mysteries! St. Bernard says: "Jesus willed that His Heart should be wounded, in order that through the visible wound we might contemplate the invisible wound of love." He willed that His Heart should be pierced so that we might enter without hindrance, and find there both a shelter and refuge. This adorable Heart, open to all will never be closed; just and sinners can take shelter there without fear of being rejected. Wounds inflicted on the dead can never heal; that in the Heart of Jesus was made by death and love, and it will ever remain open to proclaim to all succeeding generations, that it was thus that the Savior loved mankind: *Sic dilexit.* This wound is a fruitful source of graces; the water which burst forth, the blood which flowed from it, are the types of the precious favors of mercy and love. Let us, then, go and there seek the assistance of which we stand in need; if we are weak, this Heart will be our strength; if we are blind, It will be our light; if we are sorrowful, It will be our consolation: Let us exclaim with St. Gertrude: "O my Jesus! my sweetest hope, may Thy divine Heart transfixed for me, be the sure refuge of my soul! I implore Thee; by Thy wounded Heart, to pierce mine with the sword of Thy love.

Christians, is not this sacred wound of the Heart of Jesus, and its last outpouring Of blood, the great resource reserved for the fearful evils of our century? Is it not time to appeal to it, to take possession of and employ it for the deliverance of the Church, of our country, of society, and above all of poor sinners? Let us enter this very day into the divine Heart; Jesus Himself invites us, saying, as He formerly did to Blessed Margaret Mary Alacoque: "Behold the place of thy abode." Let us there remain for the rest of our lives, so that at death we may be able to say with Father de Ravignan: "How glorious a gate by which to enter heaven is the wound of the Heart of Jesus!"

EXAMPLE

Towards the end of the eleventh century our forefathers, obedient to the voice of the Sovereign Pontiff, formed the noble design of checking the barbarity of the Turks, who threatened to overrun Europe, and to deliver from their power the sepulcher of Jesus Christ. After several splendid victories the Christians took possession of Antioch, the capital of the East, where however they were soon besieged by the Prince of Mossoul at the head of three hundred thousand men. Driven to desperation by hunger, the hitherto brave soldiers felt, for the first time, their courage give way. It is related, in the history of the Church, that a holy priest of Marseilles, named Bartholomew, was inspired to seek in a particular spot for the lance which pierced the Heart of the Savior, the finding of which would be a certain pledge of the complete triumph of the Christians over the enemy's forces. The lance was found, and preceded by this glorious token of victory the Crusaders issued forth from Antioch. At the sight of the sacred spear the Turkish troops were seized with a sudden panic; the weapons fell from their hands, they fled on all sides, and the countless dead that lay on the ground testified to their entire defeat.

From whence had the lance of Calvary drawn its strength and power? From the Heart of Jesus, which it had pierced; from that precious Blood which it had caused to flow, and with which it was empurpled. O happy lance! had I been in your place, I should never have wished to leave my Savior's side; I would have said: "This shall be my rest forever." But what wonders will not the Heart of Jesus effect when It deigns to dwell in our own hearts in Holy Communion? By It we shall conquer all the enemies of our salvation, and obtain the crown of the blessed in heaven.

PRAYER

O Heart of my beloved Jesus! the Refuge opened for me by the lance, and where I need no more fear either divine vengeance or the fury of hell; permit me to hide myself in Thee, and there forget the world and myself; there let me rest after the weary toils of life, and there let me lose myself for time and eternity. Amen.

EIGHTH DAY

THE WATER AND THE BLOOD OF
THE HEART OF JESUS

WHEN the soldier Longinus had withdrawn the point of the lance which had opened the Heart of Jesus, there was seen to issue from that deep wound, *water and blood.* Even now, if we contemplate, with the eyes of faith the sacred image of this adorable Heart, that touching pledge of the love of Jesus for us, we shall see, flowing from that mysterious wound, drops of water and blood. The water flows in order that man may be born again to the life of grace by Baptism, of which it is the type. "*I will pour upon you clean water and you shall be cleansed, and I will give you a new heart and put a new spirit within you.*" Ezech. 36:25-26. St. Augustine assures us that this miraculous water has also the power to assuage the burning thirst of the passions of men. "It is not only," says he, "a salutary bath to cleanse souls; it is also a draught which refreshes and quenches their thirst." O good Jesus! "give me this water," so that I may drink and suffer thirst no more. The blood flows from the Heart of Jesus to effect our justification; its voice reaches to the throne of God, not to call for vengeance, but to ask for pity and mercy, and, at this voice, divine justice is appeased and looks down on us with love. "O sweet wound!" exclaims St. Bonaventure, "gentle wound of my Savior! what can be more wonderful! His death gives life, His wounds heal, and His blood redeems souls." It is the blood of the Heart of Jesus which still flows each day in the chalice on our altars, and gives life and grace. Yes, that sacred wine "springing forth virgins," and rejoicing souls, is the blood of Jesus. At the holy table it empurples our lips, it circulates in our veins in such a manner that, according to the beautiful expression of a holy father of the Church, we contract with Jesus Christ a glorious consanguinity. Oh! let us often hasten to drink of the chalice of salvation, and be inebriated with this divine blood.

Christians, let us repeat frequently during the day, as an ejaculatory prayer, the beautiful words of St. Ignatius: "Water from the side of Christ, cleanse me: *Aqua lateris Christi, munda me.* Blood of Christ inebriate me; inebriate me with thy love: *Sanguis Christi, inebria me.*" And when you kiss your crucifix, press your lips to the wound of the Sacred Heart, as if to draw from thence the last drops of Its blood.

EXAMPLE

Tradition relates that the soldier Longinus, who dared to plunge his lance into the Heart of Jesus, was partially blind. This misfortune, which he had endured for several years, was the result of long and severe sufferings. As he withdrew his spear, a drop of divine blood fell on his face, and at the same moment his sight was restored; his soul at the same time was illuminated with the light of faith, and his heart was filled with love for the God whom he had just outraged. Oh! wonderful vengeance of the Redeemer; He cured miraculously both the soul and the body of the executioner. Longinus was not ungrateful for so great a favor: obliged to guard the Savior's tomb after His burial, and, therefore, a witness of the resurrection, he published everywhere all he had seen and heard.

The Jews being unable to corrupt him by gifts and promises, obtained an order from Pilate that he should be put to death, and two soldiers were sent to kill him. Longinus, when he heard the decree, leaped for joy, happy to shed his blood for Him whose blood had cured and sanctified him. He asked for a white garment in which to celebrate the feast of his heavenly nuptials, and having embraced and blessed the two friends who accompanied him to the place of execution, he was beheaded. Such was the edifying death of him, who had been first the executioner, and then the apostle of the Heart of Jesus.

Oh, marvelous power of the blood which gushed from that sacred wound! If one drop alone possessed so great a virtue, what may we not hope for from that inexhaustible fountain which flows unceasingly on our altars!

PRAYER

O Heart of Jesus! how much hast Thou loved me! What would have become of me if I had not been redeemed by Thy precious blood? Alas! I should most certainly have been lost. Oh priceless balm, springing from the fountain of infinite love! Sweet Savior continue to sprinkle me with the dew of Thy saving blood, so that it may purify me more and more, and obtain for me the glory of heaven. Amen.

NINTH DAY

THE CROWN OF THORNS OF THE HEART OF JESUS

IF you contemplate attentively a representation of the Sacred Heart of Jesus, you will notice that It is encircled with a crown of thorns; thus was It depicted in the apparition to Margaret Mary Alacoque. On the day of our Lord's bitter passion, the soldiers platted a crown of thorns and pressed it with violence on His sacred head. This was, without doubt, one of the most insulting and cruel tortures which the Redeemer had to suffer in His passion. But we may well believe that these torments sprang from the Heart of Jesus, and fell back again upon It with crushing weight; for the heart is the seat of suffering as of love. The crown of thorns lacerated His Heart before piercing His sacred head. "And these thorns," says a pious writer, "were our innumerable sins, whose fearful punishment He had taken on Himself; the ingratitude of mankind who would despise His tenderness; the multitudes of those who would be lost in spite of His efforts to save them." Ah, yes, all the sins and crimes of the whole world are so many sharp thorns, which pierce and tear that adorable Heart. Nevertheless, Jesus accepts, with resignation, this bleeding crown for love of us. Oh, how dear to us should be this Sacred Heart, thus crowned with a royal diadem, placed on the altar of the cross, and consumed as a perpetual victim by the sacred fire of His love! How far more eloquently than a crown of roses does this crown of thorns speak to our hearts, and teach us to understand the burning charity of the Heart of Jesus! Oh, with what transports of love should we not cry out: "Heart of Jesus, pierced with thorns, have mercy on us." *Cor Jesu, spinis transfixum, miserere mei.*

Christians, Jesus would teach us by this mystery, that devotion to His Sacred Heart is not a devotion of sentiment, but a practical devotion which should produce in us a love of the cross and of suffering; for, as St. Bernard says: "Is it not shameful to be a delicate member of a head crowned with thorns?" Is it not a revolting contrast to see the Saint of saints in agony, and we reveling in pleasures? Jesus delivering up His head and His Sacred Heart to thorns, and we devoting ourselves to the delights and joys of this world? This mystery teaches us also humility; for the ignominious crown which Jesus wore, is the condemnation of the diadem of pride and ambition which excites our desires. He wished to show us how He loves humble souls who do good in secret, and seek not the eyes of creatures and human glory; for them the practice of virtue is sufficient. O my beloved Jesus! Jesus crowned with thorns, imprint deeply in my heart and soul these great and saving truths.

EXAMPLE

On the Feast of the Assumption, many hundred years ago, a celebrated queen said to her two daughters: "Put on your most beautiful dresses and your crowns of gold, and let us go down together to the town, and hear Mass at the Church of Our Lady." The two princesses dressed themselves as their mother had ordered, and entering the church they knelt down opposite a crucifix. At the sight of the figure of her Savior, naked, bleeding and dying, the youngest princess took off her crown and all her ornaments and prostrated herself on the pavement of the church. Her mother, surprised at her conduct, was about to express her disapproval, when the young girl, with a touching accent, addressed her thus:

"Behold, before my eyes, my king and my God, the sweet and merciful Jesus, who is crowned with sharp thorns, naked and bleeding, and shall I, a wretched sinner, remain before Him wearing a crown of gold and precious stones? My diadem would be a mockery in the presence of His." And she wept bitterly; for the love of the heart of Jesus had already wounded her tender heart. The young princess grew up, choosing always the crown of thorns offered by Jesus in preference to that of gold and jewels held out by the world, and, in after life, she became St. Elizabeth, Queen of Hungary.

Learn from this story, O Christians, that in order to deserve the crown of glory in heaven, you must here on earth wear the crown of thorns; the one must precede the other.

PRAYER

O Jesus crowned with thorns! from henceforth I will accept, with patience, all the interior and exterior sufferings which it may please Thee to send me. Nature may rebel, and I may, perhaps, say like Thee, in the Garden of Olives: "Father, let this chalice pass from me." But love will quickly make me add: "Not my will, my God, but Thine be done." Amen.

TENTH DAY

THE CROSS OF THE HEART OF JESUS

WHY does our Lord show us His Heart surmounted by a cross? It is to remind us that the whole of His passion was summed up in His Heart, which was the seat of suffering as of love. The sufferings of His body were indeed great; the most holy victim was insulted, torn, wounded in a thousand ways. "From the feet to the head, His body was but one wound." And be assured, that the sufferings of His soul, the unseen wounds of His Sacred Heart, were still greater. The cross had its place in His heart before it was erected on Calvary; for, during His life, He burned with the desire to be baptized with the baptism of blood He was to receive on the cross. "*I have a baptism wherewith I am to be baptized: and how am I straitened until it be accomplished?*"Luke. 12:50. Yes, it was His Heart that first suffered, which was filled with bitterness, was torn and sacrificed. Listen to the cry of anguish that was heard in the garden of Olives: "*My soul is sorrowful even unto death.*"

Oh, how overwhelmed, how crushed must this tender Heart have been for Him to give utterance to such words, He who was so courageous under suffering; and let us not forget that the love of Jesus for us was the cause of all He endured. "*He loved us and gave himself for us.*" "O Lord!" exclaimed the seraphic St. Francis of Assisi, "it was love that caused Thee to descend from heaven to earth, and induced Thee to pass in the world as one despised. In Thy life and death Thou didst show forth a boundless love; it was love that raised Thy cross, and love nailed Thee to it; Thou wert its slave and victim!"

Christians, the cross is the daily bread that your heavenly Father fails not to provide for His elect. "Without the cross and the Blessed Sacrament I could not live," were the words of Blessed Margaret Mary; and truly each day our hearts need a certain amount of suffering to detach us from this miserable world and conform us to Jesus, our head. Refuse not then this *cross*, these *thorns*, these *nails*, which make your life a painful martyrdom; for each wound of your heart, each torment of your soul, increases your likeness to the crucified Redeemer. Accept, as coming from the hand of your Lord, the cross He gives you to carry; the soul which knows the value of the cross, delights to suffer, and love softens suffering by remembering that HEAVEN IS ITS REWARD.

EXAMPLE

A pious and devoted mother was at the point of death; her cure was hopeless unless she submitted to a fearful operation, which the surgeons recommended her to undergo. Wishing to live for her son's sake, but above all in order to secure the salvation of her only child, the courageous woman placed herself in the hands of the operators. Her son, at her desire, was present, and she witnessed, without shuddering, all the preparations for the dreadful ordeal. At that period the producing of insensibility, through the agency of chloroform or ether, had not been discovered; even if it had, she would most probably have refused to place herself under its influence; she possessed a spiritual opiate more powerful and efficacious.

The terrible operation began; not even a sigh was heard, nor did a cry escape her; but just at the finish, when the sharp edge of the knife approached too near the heart, the poor woman moved slightly, and gently murmured: "O my God!" It was then that the son, in a frenzy of grief, at the sight of the lacerated breast which had nourished him, uttered a blasphemous imprecation. "My son," said his mother, "be silent; you give me more pain than the operators, for you insult Him who strengthens and consoles me;" and opening her hand she showed him a small crucifix she held, to which she owed the courage she had shown.

After several months of great suffering, this heroic woman died, blessing her son, and saying to him: "Keep my cross, it has given me such consolation." The crucifix has ever since been reserved respectfully in the family, and it became for her son the most precious remembrance of his pious mother. Christians, afflicted souls, preserve the cross of the Heart of Jesus, and it will comfort and save you.

PRAYER

O Jesus! when I meditate on the motives which should induce me to love and attach myself to the cross, I feel ready to embrace sufferings of every kind; but when they present themselves, I am dismayed and my courage forsakes me. Sometimes even I give way to impatience, murmuring and discouragement. Grant me grace, O Jesus! to be resigned and patient under all the afflictions it may please Thy divine providence to have in store for me. Amen.

ELEVENTH DAY

THE FLAMES OF THE HEART OF JESUS

WHAT strikes us most in contemplating the Sacred Heart of Jesus are the flames which consume and surround It. These mysterious flames cannot be contained even in that burning Heart; they escape through the wound, pass around the cross and among the thorns, covering and penetrating It completely. In a word, it is a burning Heart, an *inflamed* Heart. And what is this sacred fire which thus consumes the Heart of Jesus? It is the love which He has for us. "I am come," said He, "to cast fire on the earth; and what will I but that it be kindled." Luke, 12:49. One day, discovering His breast to Margaret Alacoque, He said to her: "My Heart, loving passionately mankind, can no longer contain the flames of Its charity; it is necessary for It to manifest Itself to them, in order to enrich them with the treasures It contains." At another time, showing her again the interior of His adorable Heart, He represented It to her as a burning furnace, glowing with flames.

Love was the life of the Heart of Jesus, was the mainspring of all Its movements, and of Its sorrows. It was love that caused Him to be born, to act, to suffer, and to weep; it was love, finally, which made Him die And in the divine Eucharist, it is love that induces Him to give Himself to us; to be our guest, our companion, our Savior, our food and nourishment. "O Lord!" exclaimed St. Gertrude, "if men but knew how Thou dost love them; if Thou wouldst but discover to them the infinite riches of Thy Heart, they would all fall at Thy feet, and would love but Thee. O mystery of infinite charity and abyss of love!"

What answer would you give, O Christians! if this good Master said to you as He did to His disciple: "Lovest thou me? Dost thou give me heart for heart, love for love?" What would be your reply? Examine yourselves, place your hand on your own heart and see if it beats with love for Jesus. Alas! its affections are, perhaps, only for creatures; how few generous souls are there, how few hearts which really belong entirely to God, to Jesus Christ. How few are they who love infinite love. How do we manage not to love that which is so lovable? Oh! let us ask of Him a *tender* love with which to love

Him, a *strong* love to suffer for Him, a *confiding* love in order to be able to lean by turns on His Heart and on His cross. Heart of Jesus, celestial flame, divine fire, destroy in us all that is not pure, and grant that our affections may be entirely thine. May we live only for love and die of love.

EXAMPLE

A priest relates the following conversion of a great sinner, in which the goodness of the Heart of Jesus is strikingly manifested:

"A young man, one of my parishioners, whose parents had given up the practice of their religion, became so impious and lawless that he scandalized even those who led bad lives. The excesses in which he indulged brought on an affection of the lungs, which, gradually developing, was slowly, but surely, leading him to the grave. I visited him and gave him many proofs of the interest I took in him; but he met my advances with blasphemies and insults, refusing even to say one *Hail Mary*. His state filled me with grief; a soul redeemed by the blood of Jesus Christ was about to perish and fall into eternal fire.

'My good friend,' said I to one of my curates,

'go at once to Paray-le-Monial; ask prayers for our poor dying man, and place his name in the Heart of Jesus.'

He set off without delay, and the next day he was at Paray-le-Monial with the pilgrims from Dijon. Prayers were said and communions offered for the lost sheep, and his name was placed in a silver heart near the altar of the Heart of Jesus. Full of hope we went again to visit the sick man. 'I prayed for you at Paray,' said the curate, 'and I have brought you a medal of the Sacred Heart.'

'I thank you,' replied the dying sinner, and, calling his mother, he asked for a ribbon, to which he attached the medal, placed it round his neck, and even kissed it with respect. 'Now, said he, 'I wish to go to confession, and it must be this very day.' He made his confession, and received all the sacraments of the Church, to the great edification of all present. Whilst I administered Extreme Unction, he said: 'Do not hurry, father, I must follow what you say, and ask pardon for my sins. Oh! how good is the Heart of Jesus in waiting for and pardoning me; if I could live longer how much I would love It." He died the following day, blessing the infinite mercy of the Sacred Heart of Jesus."

PRAYER

O Heart of Jesus! Thou dost always love us, notwithstanding our sins and innumerable crimes. In Thee love is stronger than death. Grant, by the assistance of Thy grace, that loving Thee with the most ardent love, we now obtain the pardon of our faults, final perseverance and eternal happiness. Amen.

TWELFTH DAY

THE FIRST DESIRE OF THE HEART OF JESUS: THE GLORY OF HIS FATHER

TO glorify God the Father, in making Him known, loved and served, such was the object of all the affections of the Sacred Heart of Jesus, the motive power of all Its actions, the end of all Its sufferings. Not only at His entrance into the world but in the accomplishment of each mystery, in each step of His career, our divine Lord repeated constantly — "*Behold me. O my Father, behold me: what wouldst Thou that I should do to glorify Thee? I have engraven this law in the depths of my heart, it shall always be my rule.*" He was not troubled about Himself, nor His concerns, nor His own personal glory. "*I seek not my own glory. My glory is nothing.*" John, 8:50-54. Oh! what admirable zeal and what purity of love! In truth, the Heart of Jesus seeks for Itself only contempt, humiliations and shame. He imposes silence on those who praise Him, hides Himself from those who seek to make Him king, whilst He hastens to meet the executioners who, on the day of His passion, bring Him chains and a cross. It was by accepting humiliations, a thorny crown, and an infamous gibbet that He honored His Father, and that the bleeding royalty of Calvary, which He so ardently desired, will establish the glory of God throughout the world. Then will He exclaim on the last day: "I have glorified Thee on the earth: I have finished the work which Thou gavest me to do." *Opus consummavi.*

Consider, Christians, that it is impossible to love God and not to feel an interest in his glory. Thousands of apostles, missionaries and heroic women, have made the sacrifice of their country, their families, their possessions, their lives even, in order that God should be known, loved and served in childhood, youth and all ages of life. It was because these noble souls knew how to love, because each day they said, with hearts filled with a holy jealousy for the honor and glory of God: "*Our Father, who art in heaven, may Thy name be hallowed, exalted and Praised. May Thy kingdom come in all hearts and command all affections, May Thy will be everywhere venerated and loved over the whole earth, as it is in heaven.*" Let us examine ourselves and see if these are also our sentiments; if we have not too often preferred our repose and our interests to the greater glory of God; if in our hearts we feel for the evils which oppress the Church and religion, so as to be able to say with the Psalmist: "*The reproaches of them that reproached Thee are fallen upon me.*" Psal. 68:10.

EXAMPLE

A religious of the Order of St. Francis, named Alphonsus, had labored successfully in propagating the kingdom and glory of God amongst the Indians. To evangelize these poor souls sitting in the shadow of death; to make them know and love the Creator of heaven and earth, was the object of his zeal and his preaching. Often was he heard to exclaim: "All for Thy glory, O my God; nothing except for Thy glory!"

After some years, he resolved to abandon his apostolic works, and retire to a solitary place, that he might attend only to his personal sanctification, He had been an apostle and a missionary, now he would become a hermit. One day as he was kneeling before an image of the Sacred Heart, and praying with great fervor, he heard a mysterious voice which appeared to come from the Heart of Jesus, and which said a him: "Your prayers are pleasing to me, Alphonsus; but your preachings and your Apostolic journeys were still more pleasing in my sight, for they caused many to bless and honor my Father. There are in India thousands of souls who neither know nor invoke His holy name; will you allow them to perish? and will you be indifferent to the glory of my Father, that glory which was the object of all my toils and sufferings?"

The religious replied, weeping: "Lord Jesus, I refuse not to labor; I will become again the apostle of Thy heavenly Father, and so long as I know there exists a corner of the earth where He is not known or loved, I shall never enjoy a moment's rest." He left his solitude and returned to India, where he honored God by the toils of his apostolate, and, finally, by the pains of martyrdom.

PRAYER

Grant, O Lord! that Thy glory may be the end of all our thoughts, words and works, and that we may take as our motto these sublime words: "All for the greater glory of God." O Jesus, kindle in us this divine zeal, that it may consume us as victims and holocausts entirely sacrificed to the fire of Thy love. Amen.

THIRTEENTH DAY

THE SECOND DESIRE OF THE HEART OF JESUS: THE HONOR OF HIS MOTHER

WHO can say what the love of the Heart of Jesus was for His Blessed Mother? As God, He loved her as the purest and most perfect of His creatures; He preserved her from all sin, and adorned her with all graces and virtues. As Man He loved her as would the most respectful, the most docile, the most submissive and affectionate of children. What favors, what sanctity must not the Heart of the Son have communicated to the Heart of the Mother during the nine months He reposed in her virginal womb, and during the thirty years of intimacy which He passed with her at Nazareth! During the time of His public ministry, it was frequently at the request of His Mother that Jesus worked His miracles, as He did at Cana in Galilee, so that the women of Israel, envious of such great glory, cried out: "*Blessed is the womb that bore thee.*" Luke. 11:27. In Heaven, He wills that His Mother should be the dispenser of His treasures, the channel by which His graces descend to earth. He takes pleasure in granting the prayers which are addressed to her, and to confirm by miracles the confidence that is shown by her servants. He wills that the Church should have for her the most profound respect, the most tender love, the most entire confidence; He loves to see her name united to His, and when a temple is raised to His glory, it is necessary in order to please Him, that its vaulted roof should give shelter to the humble altar of Mary. Finally, He wills, that wherever the Son is adored, the other also should be honored. "*Invenerunt puerum cum Maria.*"

Christians, if we wish to please Jesus, let us love and respect Mary; let us love her as dutiful children love their mother; she has for us all the tenderness and devotedness of a parent; her heart, like that of her Son, is an abyss of love and mercy. In our devotion, let us never separate the honor of Mary from that of Jesus; let us honor and love them both with all fervor; they were always closely united, let us not, in our affections, separate them. Let us address our petitions to God the Father through the Heart of Jesus; let us appeal to Jesus through the heart of Mary; we shall obtain all from the Father through the Heart of Jesus, and all from the Son through the heart of the Mother. Let us delight to repeat frequently the touching invocation:

Jesus, meek and humble of heart, have mercy on us!

Immaculate heart of Mary, heart like to the Heart of Jesus, pray for us!

EXAMPLE

During the fatal war of 1870, between France and Germany, a virtuous and only son, when on the point of starting to join the army, placed himself under the powerful protection of the Sacred Hearts of Jesus and Mary. His good parents had also placed in this twofold refuge their hopes for the preservation of a child so dear, and whom they looked to as the stay and support of their old age. As it always happens these hopes were not deceived. The young man, a captain in the army of the Loire, encountered the greatest dangers, he was exposed to the fire of the enemy's cannon, and saw blood flowing on every side, and yet he received no wound. He devoted himself day and night to nursing a soldier ill of smallpox, and he was preserved from the contagion. In a word, under every circumstance, Jesus and His holy Mother watched over this faithful servant with the tenderest care, and he on his side, in the midst of the toils and perils of war, never failed a single day to recite his rosary; and protected by the Sacred Hearts he returned safe and well to his family.

To mark their sense of this favor, the relatives of the man placed a slab of white marble in the Chapel of the Blessed Virgin, bearing in golden letters this inscription: "Gratitude to the Sacred Hearts of Jesus and Mary, who have preserved and restored a beloved son to his family during the war of 1870." Under every circumstance, in every danger let us invoke Jesus and Mary, let us take refuge in their Hearts and we shall always be safe.

PRAYER

O Heart of Jesus, grant that I may be always the favored child of the most holy Virgin! Inspire me with the most tender and filial confidence towards her, and give me the grace to invoke her unceasingly. Grant that her blessed name, united to Thine may be always on my lips, that thus living here below with Jesus and Mary, I may one day behold them in heaven. Amen.

FOURTEENTH DAY

THIRD DESIRE OF THE HEART OF JESUS: THE SALVATION OF SOULS

CONSIDER that the Heart of Jesus burns with an immense desire to save our souls, and to make them eternally happy. Yes, to save our souls, this is the object of His divine mission the end of the Incarnation; it is for this that He descended from heaven, took the form of a servant and the name of Savior. St. John says: "*God sent not His Son into the world to judge the world, but that the world may be saved by Him.*" (John 3:17.); and "*through Him to reconcile all things to Himself, making peace through the blood of His cross, both as to the things on earth and the things that are in heaven.*" (Colos. 1:20.) "*Neither is there salvation in any other. For there is no other name under heaven given to men, whereby we must be saved.*" (Acts 4:12.) To save our souls, such was His office, His great work for three-and-thirty years. His examples, lessons, miracles, sacraments, sufferings, His life and death, all were directed to our salvation. "*Propter nostram salutem.*" To save our souls was the object of His sacrifice: "Christ hath loved us, and hath delivered Himself for us, an oblation and a sacrifice to God for an odor of sweetness. He ended His life in the midst of the most terrible torments, exclaiming that He thirsted for the salvation of men "*Sitio!*" "I thirst." Finally, it is for our salvation that Jesus gives us His Eucharistic body, the pledge of eternal life, and His divine Heart; the sacred ark where we may all enter, and find protection and salvation. He says: "My Heart desires to manifest Itself to men, so that they may enrich themselves with this precious treasure which I disclose to them, and which contains sanctifying graces capable of rescuing them from perdition, and of saving them all." Oh! how many mysteries are there not in the burning love of Jesus for our souls, what an immense desire to save us all: can we ever sufficiently thank Him for such love?

Christians, help the Heart of Jesus to quench the burning thirst which consumes It. Alas! thousands of souls are lost, whilst you are enriched with all sorts of spiritual favors; endeavor to bring them back to God by your prayers, your good works, and example. This was what the saints did with such admirable zeal, and it was revealed to St. Teresa, that her prayers had converted to God many thousands of Indians. Church history relates that a single slave in the fourth century converted the whole of the Iberian nation. An easy way of contributing to the salvation of souls, is to join the admirable association of the Propagation of the Faith, which snatches so many victims from the devil and hell, and opens to them the gates of heaven. Let us love this beautiful work and spread it around us, and we shall save many souls.

O Jesus! give me the heart of an apostle, enkindle in me the fire which consumes Thine own.

EXAMPLE

In the year 1821, a pious young woman in the city of Lyons, was moved with compassion on hearing of the sufferings and destitution of the French missionaries in heathen lands. One evening, whilst her companions were playing at cards, she was musing on the object she had at heart, and she asked for the money won at the game to help the missionaries. Seated quietly by the fire, she wrote down in pencil on a card, the simple and fruitful plan of the propagation of the Faith, and little by little, she induced the needlewomen and servants of the town to join in her work. The first year she collected fifteen hundred francs; these details were given by the foundress herself.

At the present time the subscriptions amount to five million francs, three millions of which are collected in France. Brought in by so many hands, the weekly penny became like the grain of mustard seed, it grew and multiplied each day. On every side, men and women, rich and poor, great and small, joined the association. If God had said fifty years ago to that young girl, as He did to Abraham, "Look at the heavens and count the stars if thou canst; the souls that will be saved by thy work will exceed them in number," would not her faith have been put to a severe test? Yet today, if still alive, she would not be able to count the millions of souls saved by the work that God inspired her to commence. Oh! how the Heart of Jesus must rejoice at this abundant harvest; how rich a reward must He not reserve to the foundress and associates of this fruitful organization! Let us then love and spread this devotional and Catholic work, and we shall save those souls for whom Jesus has shed His blood.

PRAYER

O Jesus! I also thirst for the salvation of my brethren. Would that it were in my power to include them all in the embraces of Thy love. Supply my deficiency, O divine Heart! make Thyself known and loved by all the souls for whom Thou hast shed Thy blood and sacrificed Thy life. Amen.

FIFTEENTH DAY

FOURTH DESIRE OF THE HEART OF JESUS: THE RELIEF OF THE SOULS IN PURGATORY

THE HEART OF JESUS cannot be indifferent to the sufferings of these poor souls; they are His elect, His favored children, the heirs of His glory, called to bless Him eternally in heaven, His spouses whom He tenderly loves. If He could suffer, He would again offer His life to pay their debts and open heaven for them. To restrain the force of His love, it needs all the wisdom and all the merciful justice of a God who has a horror of the least stain. He can no longer suffer, He cannot die again; but from the Tabernacle, where love keeps Him a prisoner, He urges all the faithful on earth to think of the souls in Purgatory, and by their prayers and sacrifices to obtain refreshment and peace for all who are in that abode of expiation. One day He said to St. Gertrude: "Each time that you deliver a soul by the offering of the Holy Sacrifice, it is as pleasing to me as though you redeemed me from captivity, and I shall know how to reward you." On the altar, where He immolates Himself, Jesus prays for them. He wills that each time this sacrifice is offered, His suffering Church should, in the Memento for the Dead, experience its effects. Further, still, and oh! how admirable are the holy inventions of the Heart of Jesus; He unites in one vast treasury all His merits, all those of His holy Mother, and the saints; and He desires that the faithful should draw liberally from this source, so as to pay the debts of these captive souls. As soon as they are freed, He Himself comes to seek them, conducts them into the heavenly Jerusalem, and inundates them with a torrent of delights. Then, clothed with the nuptial garment, they can follow the Lamb and unite with the choir of the elect in saying "*To Him that sitteth on the throne and to the Lamb, benediction and honor and glory and power forever and ever.*" Apoc. 5:13.

Can, then, our hearts remain indifferent to the sufferings of the souls in Purgatory? Can we close them to the supplications of these prisoners who implore their liberty, these poor exiles who demand their country? From the depths of that burning abyss, they cry out to us: "*Have pity on us, at least you our friends.*" Job.

19:21. Let us not forget that it is a father or mother who is, perhaps, suffering for having loved us too much. It is a brother, it is a sister, whom we have sworn never to forget. It is a friend who has loved us much, and whose only hope is in us. Let us hasten to satisfy divine justice for them by our prayers, by our good works, by the offering of the Holy Sacrifice, by our communions, and by gaining indulgences. When, through our suffrages, they are admitted into heaven, they will become our most powerful intercessors. "*It is, therefore, a holy and wholesome thought to pray for the dead that they may be loosed from their sins.*" 2 Mach. 12:46. Heart of Jesus give them eternal rest!

EXAMPLE

Father Lacordaire, in a letter addressed to a lady of the world, relates that a Polish peasant was, at his death, condemned by the justice of God to the expiatory flames of Purgatory. His devoted wife ceased not to pray for the repose of his soul; but thinking that her prayers were not sufficiently powerful, she wished to have recourse to the Sacred Heart of Jesus, and have Mass celebrated for the deliverance of him whom she mourned.

Being poor, and not having wherewith to make the offering, which is customary, towards the support of the priest who says the Mass, she went to a rich person, who was not only a philosopher, but an unbeliever, and humbly asked him to help her; the gentleman felt compassion for her and gave her some money. The widow lost no time in having Mass offered for the soul of her husband in the chapel of the Sacred Heart, and with great fervor received Communion for the same intention.

A few days after, God permitted that the deceased peasant should appear to the rich man and say: "I thank you for the alms you gave towards the offering of the Holy Sacrifice; this Mass has delivered my soul from Purgatory, where it was detained, and now, in gratitude for your charity, I am sent by our Lord to tell you that your death is near, and that you should be reconciled to God." The rich man profited by the warning, was converted and died shortly after, in the most edifying dispositions. Let us often recall those words of Scripture: "It is a good and wholesome thought to pray for the dead that they may be loosed from their sins."

PRAYER

O Lord Jesus! these poor souls belong to Thee; they loved Thee on earth, they still love Thee amidst the flames of Purgatory; by the merits of Thy cross and Thy divine Heart, deliver them from that abode of expiation. Above all, deliver the souls of my relations, my friends and benefactors, so that, united to the choirs of angels, they may praise and bless Thee through all eternity. Amen.

SIXTEENTH DAY

FIFTH DESIRE OF THE HEART OF JESUS: THE PROPAGATION OF THE DEVOTION TO HIS SACRED HEART

"OUR LORD," said Blessed Margaret Mary, "manifested to me the treasures of grace and love, which He would bestow on those who would consecrate and sacrifice themselves, in order to procure for His Sacred Heart all the love and glory which was in their power; treasures so vast that it is impossible for me to describe them. Our Savior also showed me the names of a great number of persons written in His divine Heart, on account of their zeal in causing It to be loved and honored, and that for this reason their names would never be effaced." The longing desires and magnificent promises of the Heart of Jesus, excited to the greatest degree the zeal of the saintly religious of Paray-le-Monial. It is not in our power to relate all the efforts, the holy inventions, the generous persistence of her ardor in propagating the devotion to the Sacred Heart. She even made a vow never to refuse any labor or suffering, however painful, that could spread this devotion. In writing to one of her superiors she thus expresses herself: "*What joy is it to me that the Sacred Heart of my divine Master is known, loved, and glorified. I live only for this end, and there is nothing that I would not endure in order to make Jesus Christ reign in all hearts; even the pains of hell itself without the sin, of which they are the punishment, would be sweet to me. O God! it is more pleasing to me, and I would rather suffer in order to make Thee known and loved, than be one of the number of the seraphic choir!*" What can equal the zeal and heroic devotedness of this holy soul! Christians, let us also labor, as far as in us lies, to extend devotion to the Heart of Jesus. There are two means of propagating it which are within the reach of all: the first is prayer; let us frequently ask of God the Father to make the Heart of His beloved Son known and honored throughout the whole world; this Heart which has procured for Him more glory than all the saints and angels together. Let us often repeat the ejaculatory prayer: "*May the Sacred Heart of Jesus be everywhere loved!*"

The second is to induce those with whom we are acquainted to practice this devotion, by making known to them its objects and advantages. A word spoken with prudence and conviction, a remark uttered in and inspired by charity, will often suffice to gain hearts for the Heart of Jesus. Oh! if the fire of divine love but animated our souls, how easily should we be able to communicate to others the ardor which we ourselves experience. St. Augustine says: "If we have no zeal, the reason is that we have no love."

Yes, Lord, I will be Thy faithful apostle and I will place my glory in procuring Thine.

EXAMPLE

Providence has reserved for this century which is one of material things and earthly interests, the example of a saint whose only thought was for heaven, and who loved but the Heart of Jesus. To give an idea of the love of God with which Monsieur Vianney, the Curé of Ars, was animated, says his historian, it would be necessary to describe all the zeal, energy, gentleness, and generosity of which a human soul, aided by grace, is capable.

He thought and spoke unceasingly of the Sacred Heart of Jesus, and his words seemed flames of love. He continually preached on the devotion, recommended it to all those whom he directed, to the sick, to the afflicted, and to poor sinners. One day, it was the morning of the beautiful feast of the Sacred Heart, he said with tears in his eyes: "Let us all go to the Heart of Jesus, to the throne of divine goodness; there flows from It love and mercy sufficient to wash away all the sins of the world. Oh! if we knew how much this divine Heart loves us, we should die of joy. The only happiness on earth is to love It and to know that It loves us."

After the example of this holy priest, of this indefatigable apostle, let us recommend and propagate the devotion to the Sacred Heart. "Let us diffuse in the world the sweet odor of the Heart of Jesus Christ," said the blessed Margaret Mary, "and we shall be Its joy and crown."

PRAYER

O Heart of Jesus! Heart infinitely amiable, and infinitely holy! to what else shall we devote our lives, if not to making Thee known? To love Thee, Lord, is not enough for us; We wish to make others love Thee. We would fain possess all hearts, so that we might place them in Thine. Give us the zeal of apostles that proclaiming Thy mercies, we may save souls redeemed at the price of Thy blood. Amen.

SEVENTEENTH DAY

THE FIRST THORN OF THE HEART OF JESUS: A SOUL IN MORTAL SIN

CONSIDER that an innocent soul is the dwelling-place of God, and that in Communion it becomes in a particular manner the abode of Jesus Christ. In the words of St. Paul it can exclaim: "I live, now not I; but Christ liveth in me." (Gal. 2:20.) Yes, Jesus is at home in an innocent soul, there He finds His delight and there He desires to remain forever. To commit a sin, a mortal sin, and voluntarily to continue in this dreadful state is to admit the devil into our soul, it is to make him our master in the place of Jesus, who at once departs, driven out ignominiously and complaining in the words of Isaiah: "*To whom have you likened me and made me equal, and compared me?*" And whilst Satan chains down this poor soul and makes it his slave, Jesus stands at the door, lovingly knocks, and breathes forth these touching reproaches: "What more could I do for thee, that I have not done?" "I planted thee a most beautiful vine; and thou hast proved exceeding bitter to me." "I shed for thee my blood even to the last drop, and what has it profited thee? I nourished thee with my own flesh, and thou hast despised, persecuted, and betrayed me. O all you that pass by the way of life, attend and see, if there be any sorrow like to the sorrow that my Heart feels at such base ingratitude. Guilty soul, if thou didst know the gift of God, if thou didst know who I am, and what I give to those who open their hearts to me." "No;" answers the sinful soul, "no, I will not have Thee to reign over me." Oh! what a cause of anguish for the tender Heart of Jesus! How this cruel thorn must make His divine Heart to bleed. "Is there no one," does He exclaim, "who will take pity on me, and will compassionate my grief, in the miserable state to which sinners have reduced me, above all in these present times?"

To this cry of distress, O Christians, let us answer with words of love and reparation. "Let us hasten to our Savior's aid, let us by our prayers, our alms, and our communions, convert sinners. St. Teresa never ceased to pray for them; she continually asked Jesus Christ for souls; and we read in her life that one day when she was praying with greater fervor, she uttered so powerful a cry, so vehement a prayer from

76

the depths of her heart, that the heavenly Spouse was touched, and revealed to her that by her petition she had just saved six thousand souls, who owed to her their salvation and whom she would one day see in heaven. Let us also ask the Heart of Jesus for souls: *Da mihi animas.* If we could but save one, only one, ours also would be saved, we should give joy to the angels, we should console the Heart of Jesus. What a happiness and what a reward! Souls, O my God! give me souls: *Da mihi animas*, and keep all things else: *Cœtera tolle tibi.* Eternal Father, look on the face of Jesus, and transform all poor sinners into saints!

EXAMPLE

During the siege of Metz in 1870, a brave captain of artillery was carried wounded to the ambulance. "Surgeon," he said, "do with me what you will, but save my life. I have a wife and children, I cannot, I will not die!" Alas! all was of no use, and it was necessary to prepare for that last great Journey; but the poor man was obdurate and would not put his conscience in order. Who was there to have pity on this soul and save it from the eternal abyss?

Another captain of artillery, a fervent

Christian, determined to render him this important service. He put on his uniform as if to pay him a visit, and approaching the bed of the dying man, said to him with tears in his eyes: "Come, my dear fellow, a soldier ought to know how to die; give your poor wife and children the only comfort which is left to them, namely, that of knowing you died as a good Christian."

He then insisted that the dying man should no longer put off his religious duties, and remained with him till the priest arrived to hear his confession. Reconciled to God, and fortified with the sacraments of the Church, the dying man exclaimed in the fulness of his joy: "I am happy, I am ready for the great review. I shall go up there unburdened and decorated; all is in order." He then kissed with a lively faith a medal of the Sacred Heart, which he had received at Rome from the hands of the sovereign Pontiff, saying: "I have never left off wearing this medal, Father; when I am dead, be so good as to send it to my wife, it will be my last remembrance, my last farewell." Thus was a sinner saved by a pious friend having pity on him, and bringing him back to the fold of Christ. Oh! if we did but know the value of souls, if we did but know the desires of the Heart of Jesus!

PRAYER

Lord Jesus, pardon the numberless Christians who disown Thy love, refuse to serve Thee, and despise Thy commandments and those of Thy Church. Pardon the unhappy sinners who voluntarily remain in this wretched state, forget their ingratitude and hard-heartedness, open Thy adorable Heart, so that copious streams of grace, mercy, and pardon may flow from It. Amen.

EIGHTEENTH DAY

THE SECOND THORN OF THE HEART OF JESUS: THE TEPID SOUL

TO be neither hot nor cold towards the Heart of Jesus which merits so much love, and has manifested Itself to the world to arouse tepid souls, to drag oneself listlessly along in the service of so good a Master, fearing little to offend Him, desiring little to please Him, to be without gratitude for His favors, without care for His glory, without zeal for what concerns Him, these are the characteristics of tepidity. What disorder is this guilty apathy in a soul which professes to honor the Sacred Heart; and what does Jesus say to such a soul? "Because thou art lukewarm, and neither hot nor cold, I will banish thee from my Heart, and I will begin to vomit thee out of my mouth." Unfortunate soul, do you hear this dreadful threat? does it not give you a terrible idea of the disgust with which you inspire Jesus, and the difficulty of your return to the adorable Heart whose indignation you have provoked? Yes, He who hastens to meet the greatest sinners, and who receives the prodigal child with tenderness, even He can no longer bear with you, but will vomit you out of His mouth. O Jesus! what, then, has this poor soul done to excite to such a degree Thine anger? Has it been guilty of the sin of scandal or sacrilege? "No, but it is without zeal for my service, without a generous love for my Heart which has loved it so much; it is lukewarm: *Quia tepidus es.* Oh! I would prefer a great sinner, capable of generous resolutions, to this soul steeped in the languor of tepidity: *Utinam frigidus esses!* I would thou wert cold. I can no longer bear with it; it excites the indignation of my Heart; it disgusts It; I will begin to vomit thee out of my mouth: *Incipiam te evomere.* Oh! is not this the greatest misfortune; is not this a more sad fate, in one sense, than that of the sinner?

Christians, if, unhappily, you are infected with this disease which so often proves fatal and which is yet so common, remember that there exists two remedies which are infallible. The first is prayer to the Heart of Jesus; He has promised that He will cure and save all those who invoke with confidence His Sacred Heart; yes, even lukewarm souls; He will cast down upon you a spark of love, and you are restored to fervor and life. Say often to your merciful Savior: O Jesus! *he whom Thou lovest is sick*, come and heal him, and He will give back to you the strength and fervor of your early years; take courage, then, and throw yourself into this divine Heart. The second remedy is to let no day pass of this beautiful month, without offering to Jesus some small sacrifice, some little effort to overcome your inclinations. He will at once reward you by the peace and joy of His love. Yes, do this and you may rest assured that not only will you be cured, but that you will no longer be in danger of the spiritual death, which is the infallible consequence of tepidity. *Hoc fac et vives.*

EXAMPLE

It was not in vain that our Lord revealed the devotion of His Sacred Heart as the great remedy for the dreadful evil of lukewarmness. Each day a happy experience confirms the truth of the divine promises made by our Lord to His servant, Margaret Alaçoque. The following incident took place, some short time ago, in a town in the north of France:

A priest, zealously devoted to the Sacred Heart, came there on a visit for a few weeks.

Month of the Sacred Heart

One day a woman, somewhat advanced in years, accosted him and begged him to hear her confession. "I am unable to do so," he replied, "for I have not the necessary faculties to hear confessions in this diocese; besides you have plenty of confessors in the town." The woman answered: "I will try to obtain for you the necessary faculties; the salvation of my soul is at stake." These words made a deep impression on the mind of the worthy priest, who agreed to meet her in the course of a few days. In the meantime he made inquiries concerning the woman, and learned that she had for years been very fervent and occupied in many good works, but little by little she had become disgusted with her way of life, had given up her pious practices, and, without as yet committing serious faults, she was adding infidelity to infidelity: she was lukewarm.

On the day appointed she came to the priest, and revealed the dangerous state of her conscience, without manifesting any determination to amend herself. The confessor, seeing in how great peril her soul was, earnestly exhorted her to pray, and spoke of the devotion to the Sacred Heart of Jesus. At these words the woman replied sharply that she did not like novelties, nor superstitious practices, which were only suitable for enthusiastic imaginations.

The minister of God ordered her to be silent, and made her promise that for eight days she would reflect for five minutes on these two questions: "What has the Heart of Jesus done for me? and what have I done for It?" After much opposition she made the promise and kept it. No more was needed: in a week's time the Heart of Jesus had transformed this languid and lukewarm soul into one full of energy and burning with zeal, and she became the apostle of this devotion in that part of the country. After some years she died, leaving behind her a wonderful reputation for charity and devotedness to the Sacred Heart.

PRAYER

Divine Heart of Jesus, I wish to love and serve Thee fervently and generously, but, alas! my fervor and piety quickly die away, and I remain without love or zeal. Oh! how many of my days have been spent in lukewarmness and tepidity! Generous Heart of Jesus, be my strength and support, and grant that in future I may always labor for my salvation with energy, courage and perseverance. Amen.

NINETEENTH DAY

THE THIRD THORN OF THE HEART OF JESUS: THE SACRILEGIOUS SOUL

CONSIDER, Christians, that, though all the sacraments emanate from the Sacred Heart of Jesus, the one in which His great love for us shines forth the most conspicuously is the Sacrament of the Holy Eucharist, so deservedly called the Sacrament of love. Nevertheless, how does it come to pass that it is the mystery in which Jesus is the most outraged by those whom He has loved to excess? A painful experience proves that sacrileges become more and more frequent in these days, when charity has grown cold, and piety is feeble and more rare. This new passion, as it may be truly called, of our Savior, though more secret and less known, is more cruel to His divine Heart than that which He suffered at Jerusalem and on Calvary. O Jesus! what crime can equal that of crucifying Thee afresh and profaning Thy adorable body, by uniting Thy spotless Heart to a heart full of corruption, to tread under foot Thy precious blood, and to renew the treachery of Judas and the plots of the Jews. O what contempt of God, and what a triumph of hell! Angels of the tabernacle, witnesses of these abominations, veil your faces with your wings, and weep bitterly. Christians, represent to yourselves, with horror, the fatal moment when the Eucharistic God enters into a sinful soul, which is like a sepulcher full of corruption. What must be the humiliation, and how sharp a thorn for the Heart of our Jesus! It would seem as though the scene of the night on which He was scourged, and the day when He was betrayed by the infamous Judas, is there renewed, and it lasts so long as the sacred species remain in the breast of the perfidious and sacrilegious traitor. O God! what will be the punishment reserved for so terrible an outrage?

Faithful souls, souls devoted to the Sacred Heart, omit nothing which can make amends to this adorable Heart, for the insults and injuries to which He has willingly exposed Himself, in order to be able to give Himself to you in the most holy Eucharist. Endeavor to repair these insults by multiplying your visits to the Blessed Sacrament; pray, weep, expiate the crimes of these guilty souls; but, above all, testify your love, for the wounds of love are healed by love alone. Hasten to make a fervent communion in the spirit of reparation, and, to supply for your insufficiency, offer the dispositions of Mary when she received the Sacred Host from the hands of St. John. Oh! may you, by the earnestness of your prayers, the ardor of your love, the purity of your heart, and the abundance of your tears, console the Heart of Jesus, for so many sacrileges and profanations. May the sweet Savior be able to reverse in your regard the words of Scripture, and say: "*I looked for one that would comfort me, and I have found one.*" May the Sacred Heart of Jesus, in the Holy Eucharist, be everywhere loved and adored!

EXAMPLE

A poor man asked an alms of St. Paulinus, Bishop of Nola. The prelate, observing that one of the beggar's hands was withered, asked him the cause. "I am the son of a widow," he answered, in an agitated voice; "from my childhood I was disobedient to my kind mother, and, as I advanced in years, I ran through all her fortune. One day, when she refused to give me the last bit of money that was left her, urged by a diabolical frenzy, I struck her with this hand, which is now withered, and she fell dead. This dreadful crime took place on the night before Maunday Thursday, when I was preparing to receive my Easter Communion. Having hidden the bleeding corpse of my poor mother, I had the audacity to approach the holy table; but, O truly dreadful miracle! no sooner had I received the Sacred Host than my hand stiffened, and, with the most terrible pains, became withered. My cries attracted the astonished gaze of the whole congregation, and, overwhelmed with confusion and shame, I fled, to escape being seen by those I knew.

From that fatal day, I wander about here and there, bearing with me this withered hand, as the just punishment of my frightful sacrilege. Willingly would I bear this temporal punishment, if I had not to expect the still more fearful pains of hell." Touched by this recital, St. Paulinus said to him: "There is in the Heart of Jesus, whom you have so grievously offended, enough compassion and mercy to pardon you. Do penance, confess your sins with deep repentance, and then make a fervent communion in reparation for your sacrilegious one."

A ray of hope illuminated the countenance of the poor sinner, and he followed the advice of the holy bishop; hardly had he received the body of the Lord with all the ardor and devotion of which he was capable, than warmth and life returned to his withered hand; he was cured. O ineffable goodness of Jesus! who pardons every crime on true repentance, and changes a traitor into a friend of His divine Heart.

PRAYER

O Jesus! I would rather die a thousand times than ever approach Thy sacred table unworthily. Before seating myself at the banquet of angels, I will prove and purify myself from all stains; then, Lord, Thou wilt descend into my soul, reign over it with joy, and find there Thy delights. Amen.

TWENTIETH DAY

FOURTH THORN OF THE HEART OF JESUS: THE SOUL WHICH COMMUNICATES SELDOM

TO unite Himself to us by communion, which was the principal end which the Heart of Jesus designed when instituting the divine Eucharist. He said: "*Take ye and eat. With desire I have desired to eat this Pasch with you before I suffer. Come, eat my bread and drink the wine which I have mingled for you. Except you eat the flesh of the Son of Man and drink his blood, you shall not have life in you.*" How do men respond to this appeal? Alas! they feel nothing but coldness and indifference for the God of the Eucharist. Strange delusion, they fly from the embrace of their tender Father, they desert the holy table, and thereby excommunicate themselves.

It is true that faithful adorers of the Sacred Heart of Jesus still remain, devoted friends who, like Veronica, endeavor to wipe His adorable face, and who receive Him frequently in holy communion, But, how small the number when compared to the multitude of impious, indifferent and ungrateful Christians whose places ever remain vacant at the Eucharistic banquet. In what a sad state are these poor souls who, for so many years, have not received their God, nor quenched their thirst at the chalice of salvation? Alas! they are dying of hunger and thirst. *Qui non manducat non habet vitam.* "*Except you eat the flesh of the Son of Man and drink his blood, you shall not have life in you.*" John 6:54. Oh! how this neglect, this indifference, this spiritual death must wound the tender Heart of Jesus; what an additional thorn for that loving Heart. Listen how He complains by the mouth of His prophet: "*I have brought up children and exalted them, but they have despised me.*" Isaiah. 1:2.

Christians, will you not be moved by the lamentations of the Heart of your Master? Take pity on Him, and whilst the crowd keeps away from His tabernacle, come and pray and weep at His feet. Let the sad example of those who abandon Him cause you to redouble your zeal, your devotion and love. Approach the Eucharistic banquet as often as possible, and ask yourself if you have not frequently missed holy communion through your own fault? Yes, love

91

Jesus for those who love Him not; visit Him in the Blessed Sacrament for those who come not near Him; and, especially, open your heart to Him for those who will not open theirs. In return may those beautiful words, which He addressed to blessed Margaret Alacoque, be addressed also to you: "My daughter, I am coming into the heart which I have given thee, so that, by thy ardent love, thou mayest make reparation to me for the injuries I have received from lukewarm and cowardly hearts, who abandon and dishonor me in the most holy Sacrament."

EXAMPLE

We read in the lives of the saints that St. Alexis, who was born of noble and wealthy parents, renounced, at an early age, all the goods of this world, and left his paternal home to embrace the voluntary poverty of Jesus Christ. He had been rich—he became a beggar. At the expiration of a few years, he returned and knocked at the door of his father's house, asking for alms and shelter. His relatives did not recognize him, want and privations having so changed his appearance that they took him for a stranger, and allowed him to take up his abode under the staircase of the castle, giving orders to a servant to take him daily a piece of bread and a glass of water. Many years passed by; Alexis saw his parents leave and enter the castle without knowing him, although he himself remembered them well.

One day he fell seriously ill and sent to ask to see his mother. Just before breathing his last, he addressed her in these words "Mother, I am Alexis, I am your child." When the poor mother recognized her son in the inanimate body of the beggar, who, for thirty years had lived under the staircase of her palace, she threw herself on his neck, and, embracing him, exclaimed, weeping: "O, my child, my dear child, I recognize you, but too late!"

How many sinners, after death, at the sight of Jesus, whom they have disowned, will cry out, in like manner: "O my Savior! O God of the Eucharist! I recognize Thee too late; I have passed thirty, forty years of my life close to Thy tabernacle, almost under the same roof with Thee, and I have not known Thee, and I have refused to receive Thee." What will Jesus answer? "And I also, I know you not." *Nescio vos.* "Depart from me." *Descedite a me.* Matt. 25:12-41. To deprive oneself of our Lord in this world, and to be deprived of Him for all eternity, O God how terrible a misfortune!

PRAYER

O Jesus! it is with a heart overwhelmed with grief that I ask Thy pardon a thousand and a thousand times, for the indifference of all those who refuse to receive Thee. From henceforth I will communicate frequently, in order to console and make amends to Thee for the neglect of others. Grant that I may always approach Thy holy table with a heart free from sin, and adorned with virtue. Amen.

TWENTY-FIRST DAY

FIFTH THORN OF THE HEART OF JESUS: THE UNGRATEFUL SOUL

IT is related in the life of St. Francis of Assisi, that, urged by zeal for the glory of God, he passed weeping through the towns and villages of Umbria: exclaiming: "*Love is not loved, love is not loved.*" If this was the cause of so lively a grief in the thirteenth century, in that age of faith when St. Francis, St. Dominic, St. Bonaventure, St. Louis and St. Elizabeth effected, by their examples, so much good, what words would now be required, and how many tears would have to be shed, to deplore the ingratitude of the present age towards the loving Heart of Jesus? Listen to the complaint He uttered: "Behold this Heart which loves men so much and which is *so little loved in return.*" Sad as the thought is it is, unfortunately, true, for how many souls are there who do not know the tender and generous love of the Heart of

Jesus for them; their number cannot be enumerated. How many others are there who have some knowledge of it and yet are not faithful in making a return for so much love. Alas! there is nothing more common in the world than ingratitude; and how this fresh and painful thorn must cause the Heart of Jesus to bleed. We have the assurance of it conveyed in the words He addressed to His servant, the blessed Margaret Mary: "*That which grieves me more than all I have suffered in My passion is the ingratitude of men. They receive with coldness and indifference every sign I vouchsafe them of my willingness to confer benefits on them.*" Who would not deplore, from the bottom of their hearts, such deep ingratitude; who would not shed tears of blood over the thought, that all the proofs given to us of the tenderness of Jesus Christ become, in consequence of our indifference and wickedness, the cause of the great sorrows of His adorable Heart!

Christians, since gratitude is one of the distinctive marks of devotion to the Sacred Heart, you should endeavor never to pass a day without recalling to your mind the blessings you have received from God; the blessings of creation, of preservation, of the call to the true faith, of the sacraments, of the Heart of Jesus, and many other particular graces. Do yet more;

thank God for all the favors He would have bestowed on you if you had been more faithful, and for all those that, in the future, will be granted to you. Thank Him for all those who, receiving His favors, return Him no thanks, or use them only to offend Him. Gratitude is the special virtue of noble and generous souls, and is a most sure means for obtaining fresh blessings, whilst, on the contrary, ingratitude dries up their source. O Jesus! give us Thy loving Heart, we will offer It to Thy Father, and this offering will fully discharge our debt of gratitude.

EXAMPLE

During the reign of terror in 1871, the prisoners of the Commune, in Paris, in the dungeons of Mazas, were preparing to make the sacrifice of their lives to God. They ceased not to repeat again and again: "V*eni, Domini Jesu!* Come, Lord Jesus." And the answer was: "Yes, behold I come quickly: *Etiam venio cito.*" Apoc. 22:20. Suddenly the doors opened, the captives did not leave, but Jesus entered.

A courageous woman, whose twofold character of American and Protestant enabled her to visit the prisoners without exciting suspicion brought to the confessors of Jesus Christ a little box, containing several consecrated hosts, which a priest had secretly given her, begging her not to fail in placing it in the hands of the captives. The prisoners were filled with joy and consolation.

"I am no longer alone," wrote one of them; "I have our Lord as my guest in my little cell; I feel as I did on the day of my first communion, and I shed tears of joy. O my God! how good Thou art! how true it is that the mercy of Thy Heart will never fail! What thanks do we not owe to the benevolent woman who has procured us so much happiness; we cease not to pray for her, and we hope that the gift she made to us may be rewarded, more especially in the time of trial." On the 24th of May, the hour sounded for leaving earth for heaven; fortified with the holy Viaticum and Jesus in their hearts, the saintly prisoners went forth to yield up their lives into the hands of God. A volley was heard, then one or two single shots; all was over, the victims were no longer victims but martyrs. Their grateful prayers were not offered in vain; the Protestant lady who had brought them the Sacred Hosts, received in return, from the Heart of Jesus, the gift of the true faith. She is now a Catholic. Happy woman! who found thus a heavenly treasure in the midst of the horrors of a siege, which destroyed so much earthly wealth. On her return to America, she was able to proclaim the gratitude of the French martyrs and the generosity of the Heart of Jesus.

PRAYER

Divine Heart of Jesus, I bless and thank Thee for all the favors that Thou hast bestowed on me, notwithstanding my unfaithfulness to grace, I thank Thee also for all that Thou hast granted to my relatives, friends and benefactors. I offer Thee in return the thanksgivings of all fervent souls, those of the Blessed virgin and the saints, and with Thy prophet I will never cease to say: "Give praise to the Lord, for He is good, for His mercy endureth forever." Amen

TWENTY-SECOND DAY

FIRST MEANS OF HONORING THE HEART OF JESUS: FREQUENT COMMUNION

CONSIDER that the object of devotion to the Sacred Heart is to inflame all hearts with love. Now the memorial of all the miracles of love accomplished by our Savior is the holy Eucharist, that divine food which He has prepared for those who fear Him; and the greatest proof of gratitude and affection that we can give is to receive Him who gives Himself to us. Sister Agnes of Jesus, of the order St. Dominic, was so convinced that the Man God, in instituting the Blessed Eucharist, had willed to enkindle divine love more and more in our hearts, that at the moment of Communion she exclaimed in a transport of joy: "Let us approach the God of love." One day she received the Sacred Host under the form of fire, which so inflamed her heart with love, that she seemed during the remainder of the day unmindful of all things else. St. Teresa, when dying, regretted she could not die of love, and her desire for Holy Communion was so great, that she would willingly have exposed her life to danger, if by so doing, she could have partaken of the Bread of angels. It is said in Scripture: "*Can a man hide fire in his bosom and his garments not burn?"* Prov. 6:27; in like manner, it is impossible that our hearts should not burn with love, if we often receive Jesus, in the Sacred Host. Pious souls, truly devoted to the Sacred Heart, eagerly desire to participate frequently in this divine banquet, and they rejoice when the days of Communion come round. With them, as with the heavenly spirits who are continually nourished with God without ever being satiated, the more they communicate, the more they desire to communicate. Blessed Margaret Alacoque used to say: "without the Blessed Sacrament I could not live."

Christians, are you animated with a great desire to communicate, or do you not feel a sort of indifference, nay, even repugnance to approach the Bread of Angels? Oh! if you did but realize the pain you cause the Heart of Jesus. Communicate in future, as often as you can, your good Master invites you. "Take ye and eat, this is my Body." Matt. 26:26. "*With desire I have desired to eat this Pasch with you.*" Luke 22:25. Communicate then often; the faithful of the early Church used to receive every day; how great was their fervor and faith. Communicate often to make reparation for the indifference, the coldness, the insults, the treachery of which Jesus complains when speaking of the Holy Eucharist. Yes, communicate often, and may you be able to say with blessed Margaret Mary: "I have so great a desire for Holy Communion, that in order to obtain it, I would willingly walk bare-footed along a paths of flames." In return you will merit to hear the consoling words which Jesus addressed to his humble servant: "My daughter, I have chosen thy soul to be for me a place of repose on earth; and thy heart shall be a throne of joy for my divine love."

EXAMPLE

In an ecclesiastical seminary of the diocese of Rouen, one of the students was distinguished for his piety and intelligence, and was generally the first in his class. The day after he had made his first Communion, he went, as was the custom, to his director, to show him the paper on which he had written his resolutions. These consisted of one only, couched in these words:

"I am resolved to continue to wear the white neck-tie of my first Communion, as long as I do not commit a grievous sin." The priest was surprised and said to him:

"I cannot take upon myself the responsibility of allowing you to keep so strange a resolution; you must go to your mother and first ask her permission." This he did, and explaining the whole matter, he pleaded his cause so well, that he was permitted to follow his pious wishes. George, for such was his name, was not satisfied with keeping only this memorial of his first Communion in order to preserve himself in the grace of God, he made a rule to receive Holy Communion every Sunday and on the principal feasts of the year.

In 1870 he finished his studies and took his degree as Bachelor in Arts. He had then completed his eighteenth year. When the war broke out between France and Germany, he obtained his father's permission to join the Pontifical Zouaves under General Charette. He had been a model of every Christian virtue at college, and he was one also as a soldier, continuing every Sunday his weekly Communion.

In the month of January, when near the town of Le Mans, the Zouaves were ordered to retake an entrenchment from the Prussians.

George distinguished himself by his bravery, and though his side was victorious, he fell mortally wounded. Immediately he asked for the chaplain and said to him:

"Father, three days ago I went to confession and Communion and I have nothing on my conscience; be so good then as to bring me the holy Viaticum. I will also ask you to do a little commission for me; go to my knapsack, you will know it by its number; there you will find a white necktie, a White ribbon, and a rosary; they are the memorials of my first Communion; be so good as to bring them to me." When the priest returned, George said: "Put the white tie round my neck," this the priest did, and having received the holy Viaticum, George added, "When I am dead, take off this necktie and send it to my mother; write to her and tell her from me, *that this necktie of my first Communion has never been stained, except with the blood I have shed for our unhappy country.*" Oh! how beautiful was such a death! was it not the result of his frequent Communions?

PRAYER

O my God! how much does my indifference terrify me, and my lukewarmness afflict me. Alas! how often have I not forgotten to eat the Bread of life; how many communions have I not missed through my own fault. Divine Jesus, grant me a great hunger and thirst for thy sacred Body and Blood; I will in future communicate as often as I am allowed, and every day if I am able. Amen.

TWENTY-THIRD DAY

SECOND MEANS OF HONORING THE HEART OF JESUS: VISITS TO THE BLESSED SACRAMENT

CONSIDER that next to hearing Mass, and receiving Holy Communion, there is nothing so acceptable to the Sacred Heart of Jesus, or so beneficial to our souls, as to visit often our divine Lord in the Sacrament of His love. Yes, both day and night, the Master is there on His throne of mercy. *Magister adest.* He is there with His Body, His Blood, his soul, and divinity, in a word the same as He is in heaven, except that His glory is veiled. He is there with His boundless love for us, He is there as the Lamb ever mystically immolated, whose Blood pleads for mercy for all poor sinners. He is there with His Heart, so good and so compassionate, so afflicted by our ingratitude, so eager to pour into our souls streams of grace. The Master is there and honors us by His loving invitation:

Vocat te. "*Come to me all you that labor and are burdened, and I will refresh you,*" Matt. 11:28. *Behold I am with you all days even to the consummation of the world,* Matt. 28:20. *My delights are to be with the children of men.*—Prov. 8:31. Every day I stretch my hands to you; come to me; my Heart overflows with graces ready to enrich you." Oh! how ungrateful and indifferent shall we not be if we refuse to listen to the call of so good a Master! Does not a devoted child love to meet its father and take pleasure in being with him; and what greater consolation is there on earth than conversing with a faithful friend? "It is impossible," says a pious author, "to enumerate all the graces which a soul receives during these visits to the Blessed Sacrament. Lights which illuminate the understanding are there obtained, or inspirations which soften the heart and graces which sanctify; so that it might almost be said, that the salvation of a soul faithful in making the daily visit to the Blessed Sacrament is secure." St. Aloysius Gonzaga, St. Stanislaus Kostka, Blessed John Berchmans, found their only happiness in being near Jesus in the Eucharist, and it was there that St. Francis Xavier sought repose after the labors of his apostolate, and gathered fresh strength to undertake new conquests. In a word, devotion to the Sacred Heart of Jesus hidden under the Eucharist veils, has always been the favorite devotion of all the saints.

Christians, examine your conscience on this point. Have you a fixed hour for visiting the most holy Sacrament? Are you faithful in keeping to it? Do you not prefer visits to your friends and acquaintances, visits which are often useless and dangerous to your salvation? In short, in your temptations, your discouragements, and afflictions, is it at the foot of the Tabernacle, that you seek comfort and strength? Resolve, from this moment, never to let a single day pass without visiting Jesus the Prisoner of love, and in these visits, propose to yourself to honor in a special manner the Sacred Heart of Jesus, and to make reparation to Him for the coldness and neglect of others. When retiring from the church, leave your heart in the holy Ciborium with the divine Host, continue in spirit to adore and love Him, thus you will be able to say with the great apostle St. Paul: "Who shall separate us from the love of Christ?"

O Heart of Jesus! may the fire of Thy divine love daily increase within me.

EXAMPLE

Some years ago, a young man was, unhappily, led astray into the paths of Jewish infidelity. Whilst still in the flower of youth, his heart was filled with dreams of glory, and, being a distinguished musician, he hoped to achieve it, by introducing on the stage the inspirations of his genius. One evening, he was asked to play the organ in one of the principal churches in Paris; and this unexpected occasion for displaying his talents was eagerly accepted by the young man. There in that church God, awaited Him, and prepared for him, not a triumph for his self-love, but a humiliation a thousand times more glorious. Already the roof of the sacred edifice reechoed the sound of the solemn chants, and the melodious tones of the organ had filled all hearts with recollection and prayer; every head was bowed and the God of the Eucharist had blessed His children prostrate in lowly adoration.

The unbelieving musician, alone, dared to raise his haughty brow before that God despised by his forefathers, but it was in vain. A mysterious and invisible hand bowed his head and humbled him to the ground. A miracle of grace was effected, the man was conquered; he knelt down a Jew, he rose up a Christian, unbelief had given place to faith. Bewildered, his heart wounded, as it were, by the Real Presence in the sacred Host, he left the church; soon the waters of baptism were poured upon him, and exchanging his fashionable attire for the coarse serge of a monk, he bade an eternal farewell to the pleasures of the world.

A living example of the power of the Blessed Sacrament, he went from city to city, and from village to village, proclaiming everywhere the love of that God who had vanquished his unbelief, and in the unspeakable joy of his happiness, repeating again and again: "The days of grief are departed. I have found peace of heart since I have tasted the delights of the tabernacle of the Lord." If you would know the name of this privileged soul, ask it at the cloister of Mount Carmel, still fragrant with the sweet odor of his memory, and they will tell you it was Father Augustine, of the most Holy Sacrament. Augustine, to remind him of his errors and wanderings; and of the most Holy Sacrament, to excite him to bless forever the divine cause of his conversion. If one single visit to the God of the Eucharist transformed an obstinate Jew into a good Christian and holy monk, what may we not hope to obtain in future, by fervent and devout visits to the Blessed Sacrament of the altar!

PRAYER

O Jesus! O incomprehensible love! since Thou art so good as to dwell amongst us, I now resolve to visit Thee frequently in the Holy Eucharist. Shower down Thy graces upon me during the happy moments of intercourse with Thee. My poor heart needs rest, and this rest may be found in Thee even here below, whilst we wait to possess it in all its plenitude in our heavenly home. Amen.

TWENTY-FOURTH DAY

THIRD MEANS OF HONORING THE HEART OF JESUS: TO SANCTIFY THE FIRST FRIDAY OF EVERY MONTH

OUR Lord, when appearing to Blessed Margaret Mary, said: "My child, be attentive to my words and to what I shall command you for the accomplishment of my designs. You must communicate on the *first Friday of every month*, so as to honor my outraged Heart." Margaret Alacoque faithfully observed this injunction, and she received at those times most abundant favors. The first Friday in each month is, therefore, a feast day established by our Lord Himself, a day on which His divine Heart expands to bestow on us copious and special graces. On this favored day, fervent souls rejoice and feel the need of drawing near to the adorable Heart of Jesus which loves man so much; of being intimately united to Him in Holy Communion; of visiting Him in the Sacrament of His love, to rekindle at the burning furnace of His sacred Heart the fire of their zeal and their desire for perfection. They also set apart this day to recollect themselves, and to examine their consciences before God as to how they have spent the last month; and they make resolutions to sanctify better the one which then commences. In many parishes in France, Benediction of the Blessed Sacrament is given on the first Friday of the month, preceded by an act of consecration to the Sacred Heart of Jesus, and in several religious communities, there is Exposition during the day, followed by Benediction. Many miracles of protection in danger, cures and conversions to God, testify that the first Friday of the month is a privileged festival, a day on which all graces can be asked for and obtained from the merciful Heart of Jesus: "This is the day which the Lord hath made: let us be glad and rejoice therein." (Psalm 117:24.) *Hæc dies quam fecit Dominus.*

Christians, since we know that the first Friday of each month is the day which Jesus has chosen, let it be for us a day of grace and recollection. A God condescends to make known to His creature what will be pleasing to Him and beneficial to us, and shall we neglect to perform it? No, it shall not be so; in the morning let us make our meditation on the riches of that adorable Heart, and ask It to instill into our souls holy thoughts, with which to occupy our minds throughout the day. Let us also hear Mass and receive Communion with all fervor, offering to Jesus the ardent love of His servant Margaret Mary to supply for our deficiencies. We should, if possible, choose a quiet time to make a review of our conduct during the past month, to ask pardon for our faults, and thank God for all His graces, concluding the day by a visit to the Blessed Sacrament, and an act of consecration to the divine Heart of Jesus. If we are faithful to these pious practices, how many favors and blessings shall we not draw down upon our souls, and transported with holy joy we shall be able to exclaim with the Psalmist: "O Jesus! Jesus! Lord of Hosts! *How lovely are Thy Tabernacles, my soul longeth and fainteth for the courts of the Lord. My heart and my flesh have rejoiced in the living God. For better is one day in Thy courts above thousands; quam dilecta tabernacula tua!*"

EXAMPLE

A few years ago, as is related in the *Messenger of the Sacred Heart*, a poor woman who had scarcely ever known the blessing of health, was at last obliged to keep her bed, being reduced to a state of complete exhaustion. The doctor, thinking she was in a hopeless condition, did not prescribe any remedy; and being forced to send her children out to work every day, the poor widow was left almost entirely alone. She used to leave her door open from morning to night, so that the neighbors and charitable passers-by might come to her aid in case of need. Her patience was wonderful, and no one ever saw her yield to impatience or sadness. One thing, however, grieved her: it was the thought of dying without seeing the beautiful statue of the Sacred Heart, which had been placed in the parish church. "Ah!" said she, "it is certain that I shall never be able to go to church again; I shall never see the Sacred Heart." Those about her replied: "Do not lose confidence; if it is necessary, you can be carried to the church."

The poor woman began a novena to the divine Heart of Jesus, and asked to have a Mass said for her on the *first Friday in the Month of May*, at the altar of the Sacred Heart, hoping to be able by some means to assist at the Holy Sacrifice. Her friends agreed to wrap her in a large shawl and carry her to the church; but this was not enough for her. She insisted on fasting so that she might go to Communion.

The first Friday in May came round, and her

daughter and a neighbor carried her in their arms to the church. After hearing Mass and receiving Communion, she heaved a sigh and exclaimed: "I am cured! Return thanks to the Heart of Jesus." She rose up and walked alone to the altar which was decorated for the month of May, where for some space of time she remained on her knees praying; she then returned to her home without support, and without experiencing any inconvenience. Her cure was complete and lasting; the poor woman restored to health became the joy and happiness of her little household, and she showed her gratitude towards the divine Heart of Jesus by never failing to communicate in thanksgiving, every first Friday of the month.

PRAYER

O Jesus! in future I resolve to keep each first Friday of the month as a festival in honor of Thy Sacred Heart. I will invoke Thee with greater confidence, I will communicate with more fervor, and Thou wilt shower down on me Thy most abundant graces and blessings. Amen.

TWENTY-FIFTH DAY

FOURTH MEANS OF HONORING THE HEART OF JESUS: TO VENERATE ITS PICTURES

"MY SAVIOR," said Blessed Margaret Mary, "has assured me that He took the greatest pleasure in seeing the interior sentiments of His Heart and love honored under the representation of His human Heart, the same as He had manifested It to me, encircled with flames, crowned with thorns and surmounted by a cross; and He desired that this *representation* should be publicly exposed, in order," she added, "to touch the cold hearts of men. At the same time He promised to pour forth abundantly on those who honored it, the treasures of grace with which His Sacred Heart is filled, and that wherever this representation should be exposed it would draw down all manner of blessings." Blessed Margaret Mary spared no efforts in having this holy image engraved and distributed everywhere. Her desire was to show it to all sinners in order to convert them, and to all the just so that they might be inflamed with love. She even painted one of these pictures with her own blood, and composed a prayer and an act of consecration, in which she gave herself to Jesus without reserve, and forever.

Relying on this solemn promise of our Savior, those who are devoted to the Sacred Heart love to venerate Its holy representations, and to distribute these pictures so that the sight of them may console and encourage all. It is related in the Acts of the Apostles that the shadow of St. Peter healed the sick; should we then be surprised that not only the Sacred Heart of Jesus, but even Its *image* is powerful enough to heal the maladies of our souls? St. Teresa wished to see it in all the places where she cast her eyes. "Being," she says, "unable to represent objects to my imagination, I was extremely fond of pious pictures. Unhappy those who lose by their own fault, the help which they might draw from them. It is evident that they do not love our Lord, for, if they loved Him, they would rejoice to see His picture, just as in the world, people are pleased to see the portraits of those whom they tenderly love."

"Christians, in order to excite your devotion, have in your room some representation of this adorable Heart, painted, so to speak, by the hand of our Savior Himself; place it where you can often see it, so that the sight of it may enkindle in your heart the fire of divine love; kiss it even with the same respect as you would the Sacred Heart of Jesus Itself. Shrink from no sacrifice in order to propagate these holy pictures; distribute them in the remotest villages, in the humble cottage of the poor laborer, so that at night, at the time of prayer, all may understand the treasures of love with which this Sacred Heart is filled for us. The more these pictures are distributed, the more the Heart of Jesus will be known and loved.

EXAMPLE

A few years ago, a loving mother, on bidding farewell to her son, leaving for the African war, gave him a medal of the Sacred Heart of Jesus, making him promise to wear it always on his breast. Faithful to his word, the young officer never laid aside this pledge of his mother's tender affection and confidence, and to it he owed his life. In that glorious campaign in which the French soldiers behaved so nobly, he was chosen, as being one of the bravest and most valiant, by the commander-in-chief, for a perilous enterprise. Entering a dangerous ravine, the troops suffered greatly from the enemy's fire; the general ordered them to charge, and, the young officer leading the way, they rushed on the Arabs who occupied the pass. His regiment was almost entirely annihilated, and he was himself hit several times; but the bullet, which struck him full in the chest, and would have caused his death, was flattened against the medal of the Sacred Heart of Jesus, and he escaped uninjured.

Full of fervor and gratitude for so miraculous a protection, the young officer never ceased to proclaim the praises of the Sacred Heart, and to publish everywhere the wonders worked in his favor. Often has he been seen to kneel at the altar with his pious mother, to receive and thank the God of victory for having preserved him from certain death, and restore him safely to his paternal home.

PRAYER

Divine Jesus, I will cherish and venerate the representation of Thy Sacred Heart, which recalls to my mind the love with which It burns for me. I will give it to my friends and relations, to the sick and afflicted as a pious remembrance. Grant that it may be for all a pledge of benedictions during life and at the hour of death. Amen.

TWENTY-SIXTH DAY

THE LAST TESTAMENT OF THE HEART OF JESUS

IT would seem that, after giving us Himself in the Holy Eucharist, Jesus had exhausted the treasures of His charity; nevertheless, at the point of death, His Heart kept for us one last proof of love, and from the cross He wished to leave us a pledge of His immense and unceasing tenderness. Ah! yes, the love of our good Jesus is, indeed, unceasing and inexhaustible; He knows not how to say: "It is enough." Yet He had already given us His words to instruct us, His sacraments to purify and strengthen us, His Heart to love us, His body and blood to nourish and quench the thirst of our souls. He was going to give us His last breath when expiring on the cross: what more could He give? Oh! His Mother still remained to Him; she was His dearest and most precious possession; her tenderness was the only earthly joy He had ever known, and it is this sweet Mother whom He bequeaths to us. From the cross, where He hung in agony, casting His eyes on Mary, standing near Him, and on the beloved disciple, He let escape from His parched lips, or rather from His Heart, these four words which have touched all hearts: "*Woman, behold Thy Son: Mulier, ecce filius tuus.*" And to the beloved disciple: "*Behold thy Mother: Ecce Mater tua.*" As if He would have said: "My Mother, I am about to die; but I bequeath to you a son; I give him to you; he will love, console and protect you: *Ecce filius tuus.* And you, my dear children, whom my disciple represents, I will not leave you orphans: I am dying, but I bequeath to you my Mother, she will love you as only a mother can love, as she loved Me: *Ecce Mater tua.*" O sublime legacy! O precious inheritance! which, alone, would suffice to reveal all the tenderness of that divine Heart. The angels of heaven received that loving testament, and Jesus sealed it with His precious blood. O Mary; thou art truly my Mother, and I am thy child!

Christians, let us accept, with gratitude, this last gift of Jesus, the gift of His Mother. Oh! how great a treasure has He not given us, for the heart of Mary is the most pure, the most holy and loving that the hand of Almighty God has formed after that of Jesus. Let us bless Jesus for this wondrous gift, and let us thank Mary; but, above all, let us love this tender Mother; and whatever be our trials or our sins, let us place all our confidence in her. Can a mother ever forget her favorite child? No, indeed, and what does our Lord say by the mouth of his prophet: "And if she should forget, yet will not I forget thee." Isaiah. 49:15. Oh! what greater proof could He give us of the love of His Heart? He gives us His Mother, and assures us that He loves us much more than she can ever love us. Glory, then, to the Sacred Heart of Jesus, our merciful Redeemer and Master, and never-ending love to the immaculate and tender heart of Mary, our Mother, the Queen of Angels.

EXAMPLE

History relates that the Tartars, having spread terror throughout Europe, besieged with a large army Kinwalous, the capital of European and Asiatic Russia. After a vigorous resistance, the city was taken by assault and sacked by the enemy, who, having massacred great numbers of the inhabitants, finally set fire to it.

When the victorious army entered the town, St. Hyacinth, a Dominican monk, was at the altar saying Mass: his religious brethren came and warned him that there was not a moment to lose, and that if he wished to save himself and his community it was necessary to fly at once, otherwise he would fall into the hands of the barbarians. He followed their advice, but, unwilling to leave the divine Eucharist exposed to the profanations of the enemy, he took in one hand the ciborium, and in the other the image of the Blessed Virgin, saying to his religious:

"Follow me, my brothers, and be full of confidence; the Sacred Heart of Jesus and the immaculate heart of Mary will save us."

He left the church, followed by the community, traversed the burning streets, and passed by the hordes of barbarians, who gazed on him with respect and admiration. Reaching the banks of the river Borysthenus, and not finding any boat there, he recommended himself to Jesus and Mary, and stepping on the water which remained firm beneath him, he crossed the river with dry feet, accompanied by all his brethren, and thus they were saved! Christians! receive the divine Host into your heart, place upon your breast the image of Mary and you will triumph over all the enemies of your salvation. Heart of Jesus, Heart of Mary, be always our hope, our love, our refuge and our salvation.

PRAYER

Heart of Jesus, give us a filial love for her whom Thou hast bequeathed to us as our Mother, with Thy last breath on the cross. Grant that her protection may be our safeguard, her example the rule of our conduct, her heart our refuge and shelter in all dangers; grant that she may be our hope during life, and at the dread moment of death. Amen.

TWENTY-SEVENTH DAY

DEVOTION TO THE AGONIZING HEART OF JESUS

THIS devotion has for its object, first, to honor the Sacred Heart of Jesus suffering during His life, and, above all, during His Passion, the greatest interior sufferings for the salvation of souls; secondly, to obtain, by the merits of this long agony, a happy death for eighty thousand persons who each day die throughout the world. Nothing can be more simple and admirable than the history of this touching devotion. About twenty years ago, a saintly religious was inspired with the desire to make it known to the faithful, and for this end he composed a little prayer for those who each day are in their agony. Approved and enriched with many indulgences by his Holiness Pius IX, this prayer was distributed everywhere, and, being translated into several languages, it became known in most Catholic countries, and has given rise to the pious associations established in many towns, the object of which is to implore of God the salvation of the dying.

It is easy to understand how pleasing this devotion must be to the Heart of God, who, leaving the glory of heaven, descended on earth to save mankind from hell; it is the means of drawing down graces of conversion on a multitude of Christians, who, in this age of indifference and impiety, do not prepare for death, think not of eternity, and find themselves in the presence of the Sovereign Judge without having once reflected on their danger. It is also a means of cautioning souls against the infernal doctrines of freethinkers, who endeavor to banish the priest from the cradle of the newborn babe, from the nuptial contract, and from the bedside of the dying. Oh! what graces of salvation has not this devotion drawn down from heaven! what comfort has it not procured for the agonizing! how many expiring sinners has it not snatched from the abyss of hell, and how many souls has it not saved from eternal fire! Blessed be the agonizing Heart of Jesus for having inspired such a fruitful, opportune and providential devotion!

Christians, pray for all who are in their agony, recommend them often to the merciful Heart of Jesus, and remember that each day eighty thousand persons fall under the sword of death, appear before the dread tribunal of God and begin an eternity of joy or woe. Alas! of this number how many thousands are in a state of mortal sin! Pray for the dying; they are your brethren in Jesus Christ; perhaps relations, friends, and benefactors, for whom you should obtain a happy death. Pray for the agonizing; one day you, too, will stand in need of prayers when you are in your agony, and you will rise victorious from your last struggle to enjoy eternal happiness. Lastly, make known this devotion to the agonizing Heart of Jesus to those who are in ignorance of it: speak of it in your families and amongst your friends, and this Sacred Heart will bless you. If, by the union and fervor of our prayers we could each day save a soul, what a rich harvest we should have stored up at the end of the year! What a pledge of our own Salvation, and what a crown for all eternity!

EXAMPLE

At the recommendation of a Protestant family, living in the town of Liége in Belgium, a young lady who had been long ill was received into the hospital. She was an excellent musician, had lived entirely amongst heretics, and although nominally a Catholic, had no idea of religion and scarcely believed in the existence of God, giving herself up to all the pleasures of the world. When anyone spoke to her of religion, she became irritable and declared that such conversations fatigued her.

The nursing sisters who were in charge of the hospital, despairing of her conversion, made a novena for her to the agonizing Heart of Jesus. On the last day of the novena, the poor sinner asked one of the sisters for a prayer book and after reading a page, exclaimed: "I will go to confession and communion."

She made her confession and communion, and from that day she said to all who came to see her: "Oh! how truly happy I am." On the near approach of death, she expressed her desire to communicate again, and during her agony she repeated with fervor the words: "My Savior, my Savior, forgive me all my sins!" peacefully expiring with the holy Name still on her lips. Thus was this poor soul saved by being recommended to the agonizing Heart of Jesus. Glory and love to this divine Heart.

PRAYER

O most merciful Jesus! full of love for souls, I implore Thee by the agony of Thy most Sacred Heart, and by the sorrows of Thy Immaculate Mother, to purify in Thy blood the sinners of the whole world, who are now in their agony, and this day to die. Amen.

Agonizing Heart of Jesus, have pity on the dying.

TWENTY-EIGHTH DAY

THE SACRED HEART OF JESUS, AND FRANCE

"GOD loves the Franks," said St. Gregory of Tours, "and it is through the Franks that He loves to manifest His power." *Gesta Dei per Francos.* All nations are equally dear to God, but France must, indeed, be an object of predilection to Jesus, because it was in France that He revealed the ineffable tenderness and infinite riches of His Divine Heart. It was in that favored country, that Jesus first manifested and proclaimed that His Sacred Heart was open to all men. How great and magnificent a gift was this and what a signal honor! On account of the wonderful apparition at Paray-le-Monial, where Jesus appeared to His humble servant, a French nun, may we not say of that privileged town, what the prophet said of Bethlehem: "Thou art not the least of the cities of Juda." To the general favors bestowed on all countries, the Savior willed to add a special one to France, the nation then called most Christian.

"My Heart wills to reign in the palace of her kings, to be emblazoned on her banners and engraved on her arms, in order to render her victorious over all her enemies and those of Holy Church. I am preparing for France a torrent of graces when she shall be consecrated to my divine Heart, and all nations shall profit by the blessings that I shall bestow on her." Jesus Himself, when speaking to blessed Margaret Alacoque of the king of France, called him *"the eldest son of my Sacred Heart."* He promised to that favored land a torrent of graces which would be a treasure and pledge of hope for that now unhappy country, distracted by her infidel children. France was the cradle of the devotion to the Sacred Heart, France was the first to receive the glorious mission of being its apostle, of propagating and defending it throughout the world by the voice of her missionaries, by the pastorals of her bishops, and the blood of her martyrs. We should bless the Lord who has loved and favored France with such privileges, and instead of being jealous of her honors, we should rejoice and exclaim: "He hath not done thus to every nation." (Ps. 147.) But, alas! we have no need to envy France. May we not tremble at her fate, for has she *as a nation* returned Jesus *love for love*? No, a culpable indifference and a proud rationalism have drawn down upon her the most dreadful punishments, and that country, according to universal testimony, is passing through the most sorrowful and critical period of her history.

Christians, let us not lose courage at the sight of the miseries which overwhelm that once privileged land, or our own loved country; let us have recourse to the merciful Heart of Jesus; it is that Heart alone that can find a remedy for the social evils we see on all sides. "How powerful is this Divine Heart," said blessed Margaret Mary, "to appease the anger of divine justice provoked by the multitude of our sins, and to avert the terrible calamities with which we are threatened." Let us beg of that tender Heart to bless our country, and to bless also and restore religion to France, that she may deserve to bear once more, the glorious title of "*the most Christian nation and eldest daughter of the Church.*" Then her brave sons will be able to cry out, as did their forefathers of old: "*May Christ reign who loves France.*" *Vivat Christus qui amat Francos!*

EXAMPLE

Paris was besieged by the Prussian army; Rome had just fallen into the sacrilegious hands of the Piedmontese, and the Communists were plotting in secret their terrible plans. Who was there to come to the assistance of the Holy Father? who was there to save France? Holy souls cried out, "It is the Sacred Heart of Jesus which will save us; let us make to It a national vow." And what was this national vow? It was a promise to offer in the name of the whole nation, the solemn expression of their repentance by raising a memorial church in Paris, dedicated to the Sacred Heart.

Paris, which had been the scene of the greatest disorders, possessed no temple in honor of the divine Heart of Jesus: in no place therefore would an expiatory church be better placed or become more publicly known. There is a spot in Paris which in former times was bedewed with the blood of St. Denis and his companions, called the quarter of Montmartre, or the hill of the martyrs, and it is there that the memorial church of France is to be built. The national vow was addressed to the Sacred Heart, because this divine Heart is the highest expression of the love of God for men; and because France has in a particular manner wounded the Heart of Jesus which has loved her so much; it is therefore to the Sacred Heart that the expression of repentance and hope should be addressed. Nothing, indeed, could be more Christian or more patriotic than such a vow; it received the blessing of the holy Father and the sanction of the French episcopate.

Alms were asked, the funds increased, and subscriptions flowed in from all sides; the first stones were laid and blessed, and already may we foresee the day, when, from the heights of Montmartre, the new Basilica will be raised, which is destined to bear testimony to the regret of the French people for the past and their confidence for the future. On its principal front is to be engraved in letters of gold, the following dedication:—

"Christus ejusque sanctissimo Cordi,
Gallia pœnitens et devota!"

Devoted and repentant France, to Christ and His Sacred Heart.

PRAYER

Remember O infinitely good and infinitely merciful Heart of Jesus, Thy love for France. Remember the blessings which Thou hast showered down on her, and Thy former mercies towards her. However guilty are her people, reject not our humble prayer, and restore that once-favored country to happiness and Christianity. Amen.

God of mercy and power, save France in the name of the Sacred Heart.

TWENTY-NINTH DAY

THE COMMUNION OF REPARATION

A FEW years ago, in the diocese of Avignon, in France, a pious practice was instituted, called the Communion of Reparation. Eagerly adopted by fervent Christians, and sanctioned by the greater number of the bishops of France, it was made known to the Sovereign Pontiff, Pius IX, who deigned to approve and enrich it with many indulgences. "The Communion of Reparation," he said, "is a divine work, destined to save society." More than a hundred thousand persons are enrolled as associates, and divided into sections of seven members; they communicate once in every week on a day assigned to each; these fervent souls offer to the King of kings, hidden under the Eucharistic veils, the tribute of homage and adoration which is refused Him by so many ungrateful men, and make reparation for the outrages committed against His love and majesty. They assume the office of comforter to Him who is the comforter of all the afflicted, and their mission is not limited to this, for, imitators of the boundless charity of that divine Master, they act as mediators between Him and guilty souls; they plead the cause of sinners, and offer themselves to Him as victims of expiation, to obtain their conversion and salvation. They are truly apostles and mediators, and by averting from the guilty the punishments of God's justice, they draw down on their own hearts graces of divine mercy.

How holy and glorious is this twofold mission, how it must console the adorable Heart of Jesus! Is it not what He asked Himself of His humble servant, Margaret Mary: "I enter into this heart of thine which I have given thee, so that by thy ardent love thou mayest make reparation for the injuries I receive from lukewarm and cowardly hearts, which dishonor me in the Blessed Sacrament." Christians, let us joyfully enroll ourselves in this fervent band of the Communion of Reparation. Let us weep over the wounds inflicted on the Heart of our Master; let us bewail the little love which is shown to Him, and on the day assigned to each, let us go to the holy table as victims consecrated to the glory of our Lord in the Sacrament of His love. Let us say to Him: O Jesus! Thou art disowned by many, but I adore Thee; Thy sacred Body and Blood are despised, but I make them my nourishment, my drink, my delight. I beg forgiveness, my God, for those who love Thee not. Could I hold in my hands the hearts of men, I would cast them all into the furnace of Thy holy love. "Father, forgive them: spare, O Lord, spare Thy people: *Parce Domine, parce populo tuo.*" It is Thy children's cry, the cry of love. Lord, Thou wilt hear it and grant pardon.

EXAMPLE

Not long ago, a zealous priest wrote as follows: "Our work of the Communion of Reparation makes rapid progress and produces abundant fruit. The communions of the associates are most efficacious in obtaining the conversion of sinners. An Englishman, a Protestant, who, on account of ill health, had taken up his abode in my parish, was reduced to the last extremity. I visited him and endeavored to persuade him to embrace the Catholic faith and thus secure his salvation.

'I was born a Protestant,' he replied, 'and I will die a Protestant.'

Despairing of converting him by arguments, I assembled the associates of the Communion of Reparation, and I implored them to ask most earnestly of the Sacred Heart of Jesus the conversion of this poor invalid, who was on the point of dying in heresy and impenitence. The associates offered their communions and prayed much for him during that day, and when I went again to see him, he said, with a sweet smile:

'I am convinced of the truth, I will become a Catholic.' He made his abjuration in the presence of several witnesses, and received the Sacrament of Baptism with tears of joy. 'Father,' he said to me afterwards, 'how happy and peaceful I feel; it seems as if I were returning to life,'

A few days later he received the Holy Viaticum and Extreme Unction with sentiments of the tenderest piety, and the archbishop administered to him the Sacrament of Confirmation. Is not this an example of the consoling fruits of the Communion of Reparation? Oh! may this admirable work be known and propagated everywhere."

PRAYER

O good and loving Heart of Jesus, we understand full well Thy sadness and sorrow! We will strive, henceforth, to offer Thee, by our fervent communions, our acts of reparation and our daily sacrifices, some small amends for the outrages Thou receivest from those who have been redeemed at the cost of Thy blood. Amen.

THIRTIETH DAY

THE THREE HEARTS

LET us, O Christians, terminate the devotions of the month of June by a meditation on the wonders of the Hearts of Jesus, Mary, and Joseph, that triple abyss of perfection and graces. Let us contemplate these three Hearts so closely united at Bethlehem, in Egypt, and at Nazareth; they were animated with the same thoughts and the same feelings, the same tastes and aspirations. Never has there been, nor could there ever be amongst three Hearts, so perfect an understanding, so deep a sympathy, so absolute a resemblance. If it is said of the first Christians that they had but one heart and one soul, *Cor unum et anima una* (Acts, 4:32), with how much greater reason may it not be said of the only Son of Mary, of His Holy Mother, and of His tender foster father! Contemplate these three perfect Hearts: that of Jesus is the Heart of a God, the tabernacle where resides the Majesty of the Most High; that of Mary is the cradle of love, where an Infant God reposed, and the pure

141

and fruitful source from which He drew His life. And what must not have been the merits, the virtues and perfections acquired by the Heart of Joseph during the thirty years of unceasing contact and intimacy with the Sacred Heart of Jesus? He could indeed exclaim with truth what fervent souls love to repeat: "At all times and in all places, I possess the God of my heart and the Sacred Heart of my God." Reflect on these three loving Hearts; they loved God more than all the Saints together: they love us also more than all our relatives and friends on earth, more than all the blessed in Heaven. No one is excluded, rich or poor, just or sinner; each has a place in these Hearts burning with love. They love us in our joys and in our sorrows, in our triumphs and in our tears; they love us tenderly, they love us always, in life and in death.

Christians, your Savior tells you that "what God hath joined together, let no man put asunder." (Mark, 10:9.) In His divine plan, God united intimately the Hearts of Jesus, Mary, and Joseph; let us, therefore, never separate them in our hearts. When adoring the Sacred Heart of Jesus, let us also bless and venerate the holy Hearts of His Mother and His foster-father Joseph; since they love us so tenderly, let us invoke them with confidence, and say often:

Jesus, meek and humble of Heart, have

mercy on us.

Immaculate Heart of Mary, Heart like to the Heart of Jesus, pray for us.

Heart of Joseph, always faithful to Jesus and Mary, intercede for us.

And when the awful moment comes for each of us, when the soul passes from this tabernacle of earth to its eternal home, may the last words on our lips and in our hearts be those cherished names, Jesus! Mary! Joseph!

EXAMPLE

A pious lady who died in 1860, at the age of thirty-two years, had a great devotion to the most holy Hearts of Jesus, Mary, and Joseph. She took a particular pleasure in often invoking the names of the Holy Family, and in teaching them to her little child when seated on her knee. In her joys and sorrows, she never wearied repeating the holy aspirations: Jesus, Mary, Joseph. Many a time were tears of devotion seen to fill her eyes whilst she pronounced those blessed names. She appeared then in a sort of ecstasy, and her heart was inflamed with devotion to the Holy Family, whom she wished, she used to say, to love in the name of all hearts.

During a long and painful illness with which

she was seized, she frequently cried out: "Jesus, Mary, Joseph, when I have suffered sufficiently, call me to you." Towards the end, being scarcely able to speak, she breathed but one name: "Jesus, Jesus." That name was her great consolation, her last cry of hope and farewell. At length, after a lingering martyrdom, she gently expired, her hand on the head of her child to bless it, her eyes raised to heaven and the name of Jesus on her lips. O beautiful and precious death! O ever blessed names, Jesus, Mary, Joseph! O Hearts burning with love and tenderness!

PRAYER

Jesus, Mary, Joseph, I give you my heart and my soul!

Jesus, Mary, Joseph, assist me in my last agony.

Jesus, Mary, Joseph, may I breathe forth my soul in peace with you.

ACT OF REPARATION TO THE SACRED HEART OF JESUS

DORABLE HEART OF JESUS, consumed with love for men and thirsting for their salvation, Heart so loving yet so little loved, deign to accept this act of reparation that we eagerly offer to make amends to Thee for the outrages, the irreverences and profanations which Thou dost receive in the adorable sacrament of the altar. Pardon, O most Sacred Heart, the forgetfulness and ingratitude of men, the abandonment and indifference with which they repay Thy immense love! Forgive us all, forgive all poor sinners! Remember not our innumerable faults, and from the open wound of Thy Sacred Side let floods of grace and mercy descend upon us. Guard and protect us, hide us in this divine wound till that happy moment comes, when in our heavenly country we repeat with the angels throughout eternity: "Glory, love, gratitude, and unceasing praise be to the most loving Heart of our Savior!"

ACT OF CONSECRATION TO THE SACRED HEART OF JESUS

MOST SWEET JESUS, fountain of love, Father of mercies, and God of all consolation! who hast vouchsafed to open to us, wretched and unworthy sinners, the unspeakable riches of Thy Heart; we Thy servants, in thanksgiving for the innumerable favors conferred upon us and upon the rest of mankind, and especially for the institution of the most Holy Eucharist, and in order to repair all the injuries done to Thy most loving Heart in this mystery of infinite love, do entirely devote ourselves and all that we have, together with all the treasures of merit acquired, or yet to be acquired by us with the help of Thy grace, to this most Sacred Heart of Thine, promising that we will promote the worship of Thy Divine Heart, as far as may be in our power.

Moreover, we choose in an especial manner the most Blessed Virgin Mary for our Mother, and in like manner deliver up and devote ourselves and all that belongs to us to her most pure heart; promising that, as far as in us lies, we will promote, according to the spirit of the Church, devotion to this fond Mother, and especially to her Immaculate Conception. We humbly beg, therefore, of Thine infinite goodness and clemency, that Thou wilt vouchsafe to receive this holocaust in the odor of sweetness; and as Thou hast granted us Thy plentiful grace to desire and make this offering, so Thou wilt also grant us the same to enable us to fulfil it. Amen.

PRAYER FOR THE CHURCH

O GOOD JESUS! our Master, deliver Thy servants from the persecutions of their enemies. Have pity on Thy people and turn their sorrow into joy. In the disordered state of society, there is no one to whom we can have recourse, unless to Thee, O God! Cast Thine eyes upon Thy Church; she mourns and Thou alone canst come to her assistance. Lord, give not over Thy servants to those who hate us, and let them not triumph over us. Remember us, O Lord, and deliver us from our afflictions, Thou who livest and reignest for ever and ever. Amen.

PRAYER TO THE BLESSED VIRGIN

O Mary! it is impossible for thee to forget us, for thou art the Mother of mercy, our life, our consolation, and our hope. O Heart so tender and so good! be not insensible to our sighs and tears. Remember only that thou art our Queen, and that we are consecrated to thee. Lead us to the Heart of thy divine Son and render It propitious to us. O Mary! console the Church and save our country!

Sacred Heart of Jesus, *have mercy on us.*
Immaculate Heart of Mary, *pray for us.*
St. Joseph, *protect the Church and pray for us.*

METHOD OF HEARING MASS IN UNION WITH THE SACRED HEART OF JESUS

At the beginning of Mass

Almighty and eternal God, it is in the Holy Sacrifice of the Mass that Thou receivest a homage worthy of Thine infinite Majesty. To render it more pleasing in Thy sight, I offer it to Thee in honor of and in union with the adorable Heart of Thy Son. He is Himself the priest and the victim who is here immolated to Thy glory. I unite myself to this divine victim; receive, O my God! the offering that I make to Thee of my whole self, together with the Heart of Thy beloved Son. Adorable Heart, I offer to Thee this august Sacrifice to honor Thine ineffable perfections, to thank Thee for all the graces which Thou hast so often bestowed on me, to ask Thy pardon for my numerous infidelities and the coldness of my heart towards Thee, and to obtain fresh graces particularly. ... Deign, O

Sacred Heart! to apply to my soul the merits and fruits of this divine Sacrifice, and accept the gift of my heart in union with Thine own.

At the Kyrie

Holy Father, have mercy on the work of Thy hands. Compassionate Heart of Jesus, have mercy on a soul which has cost Thee so much. Holy Spirit, have mercy on a heart which is Thy sanctuary, and which Thou hast filled with Thy gifts.

At the Gloria in excelsis

My voice is unworthy to be heard by Thee, O my God! but united to the Sacred Heart of Thy Son, I offer Thee adoration, thanksgiving, and praise. Honor, glory, and dominion to Thee, O Lord! and to the adorable Heart of Jesus for ever and ever.

At the Collects

Lord Jesus, who hast opened to Thy Church the treasure of the ineffable riches of Thy Heart, grant that we may return love for love to this adorable Heart, and by our humble adoration make amends for the insults It has suffered, and still suffers daily from the ingratitude of men; who livest and reignest with the Father and the Holy Spirit, world without end. Amen.

At the Epistle and Gospel

Jesus, when expiring on the cross, uttered a great cry as if to call all men to Himself. A soldier, with one stroke of his spear, opened a wound in the sacred side of the Savior, from whence streamed blood and water. St. Bernard says, that Jesus was wounded by the soldier's lance, because His Heart had been already wounded with the dart of love for the salvation of men. O loving wound! exclaims St. Bonaventure, it is by thee that I am able to penetrate into the bowels of the charity of Jesus Christ. The gate of heaven is now open, and the flaming sword which guarded its threshold has been turned aside by the lance! Happy lance! which deserved to be chosen to inflict so sweet a wound! Had I been in the place of the lance, I would never have left the Heart of Jesus, and I should have said: this shall be my rest forever and ever; here will I dwell for I have chosen it.

At the Creed

I believe, O my God! the truths that Thou hast revealed, and all those that Thy Church proposes to my belief. I declare that I will live and die in this holy faith. Grant, O Heart of Jesus! that my life may be conformable to my belief, and that my faith may always be animated by good works. May I never be ashamed to act as a Catholic, and may I maintain by my works, and above all by my conduct, the interests of Thy holy religion.

At the Offertory

Look down, O all powerful God! on the Sacred Heart of Thy beloved Son, which we offer in union with the priest, as a victim worthy of Thy greatness, as a satisfaction which exceeds all our debts, as a supplication which will admit of no refusal, and an offering which Thou canst not worthily repay but in giving Thyself to us.

Accept, O Eternal Father, this Heart so pure and holy, to supply for all that Thou requirest of me, since I have nothing that is worthy of Thy acceptance but Jesus, my Savior, whom Thou hast given me in this Holy Sacrifice.

Month of the Sacred Heart

At the Preface

In union with the saints triumphant in heaven, with the Church and all the faithful on earth, I offer Thee this great sacrifice, and I enter, O Lord! into the sanctuary of Thy Heart to be consumed by the divine flames of Thy love, and to adore Thy sanctity through the sanctity of the Sacred Host which will be offered to Thee. I unite my heart and my soul to the celestial spirits, saying with them; Holy, Holy, Holy, Lord God of Hosts; the heavens and the earth are full of Thy glory, Have mercy on us and save us, O eternal King. Hosanna in the highest!

At the Canon

We adore Thee, O eternal Father! and we beseech Thee, by the precious Heart of Thy Son to receive this oblation by the hands of Thy priest, for all the Catholic Church, for our pastors and superiors, for our relations, friends, and enemies, imploring Thee to grant them a firm and strong faith, truly Christian conduct and a full and perfect union with Thee in glory; grant also, O Lord! help and assistance to the souls who are suffering in the cleansing fires of purgatory; above all, have mercy on those who

153

have been the most devoted to Thy adorable Heart and to the heart of the glorious Virgin Mary: deliver them from those burning prisons and listen favorably to our prayers; we hope for these graces by presenting to Thee the one, living, true, and eternal victim.

At the Elevation

My eyes see not this ineffable miracle, but my faith manifests it to me. The same Body which was delivered up for me, the same Blood which was shed for the remission of our sins, is really present on the altar. I firmly believe it. O divine victim! O God of love! O hidden God! I annihilate myself in Thy presence. I adore Thee under the appearance of bread and wine with which Thy love veils Thy Majesty. Thou art in the Sacred Host as truly as Thou art on the cross, and as Thou art now in glory at the right hand of Thy Father. O precious Blood! which streams from the Heart of Jesus, I adore Thee. Source of grace and mercy, flow into my heart to cool the fire of my passions, and to wash me from all my iniquities.

At the Memento of the Dead

O most merciful Father! in the name of Thy

154

Month of the Sacred Heart

beloved Son, have mercy on the faithful departed and, above all, on the associates of the Sacred Heart; in Thy clemency, grant them pardon and perpetual rest, so that they may bless, praise and glorify Thee eternally with Thy saints in glory.

At the Pater Noster

O Jesus! may Thy divine name be blessed and hallowed by all creatures; may Thy precious Blood shed for us on Calvary, purify us from all stains of sin, and strengthen us against the dangers of our salvation. O Jesus; may Thy Sacred Heart be our refuge, our shelter and our shield during life and at the hour of death. O Jesus! deliver us from all evil by opening to us the bosom of Thy love. Amen.

At the Agnus Dei

Divine Lamb, it belongs to Thee alone to take away the sins of the world. Take away and detach from my soul all that stains it; I truly detest my sins; in the name of Thy Sacred Heart, have mercy on me and give me peace, so that I may praise and bless Thee for all eternity.

At the Communion

O Jesus! King of all hearts, place Thyself as a seal on my heart and on my arm: on my heart, to close it against all earthly objects, and to direct all its affections and movements to Thee; on my arm, so that all my actions may have no other end but the glory and love of Thy Sacred Heart.

O Jesus! grant that my eyes and heart may remain ever fixed on the wound of Thy adorable Heart.

O Jesus! give me to drink of that water of which Thy Heart is the source, so that I may never more thirst.

I have found the Heart of my King, of my brother and Savior: what more can I desire in heaven or seek on earth?

After the Communion

Soul of Christ, sanctify me. Body of Christ, save me. Blood of Christ, inebriate me. Water from the side of Christ, wash me. Passion of Christ, strengthen me. O good Jesus! hear me, hide me within Thy wounds. Permit me not to be separated from Thee; from the malicious enemy defend me; at the hour of death call me and bid me come to Thee, that with Thy saints

I may praise Thee forever and ever. Amen.

At the last Prayers

Whilst honoring the remembrance of Thy meek and humble Heart, grant, O Jesus, that we may learn of Thee to be meek and humble also, so that we may obtain the peace which Thou hast promised, and find rest to our souls; Thou who being God, livest and reignest with the Father and the Holy Spirit, world without end. Amen.

At the Blessing

Praise, honor and glory to Thee, O Jesus, who having blest Thy disciples, didst ascend gloriously to heaven, where Thou sittest at the right hand of the Father; deign to bless us Thyself as Thou wilt bless the elect at the last day. Amen.

At the last Gospel

Almighty and eternal God, who by an infinite love hast established Thy Son as the only mediator between mankind and Thee, I beg of Thee to receive favorably this adorable Sacrifice. Remember not my want of fervor and my negligence in offering it. Lord, suffer me not to be separated from Thee; bless me, grant me Thy grace to serve Thee faithfully in all things even to the end, and grant that after this life, I may deserve to praise and glorify Thee eternally with all the blessed in heaven. Amen.

St. Margaret Mary Contemplating the Sacred Heart.
—Corraro Giaquinto

SHORT ACCOUNT OF
BLESSED MARGARET MARY
ALAÇOQUE.

Extracted from the Apostolic Brief for her beatification in 1864.

ORN of a noble family at Lauthecourt, in the diocese of Autun in France, Margaret Mary Alacoque was distinguished even in her childhood for the docility of her disposition and the regularity of her conduct, so that her relations were led to believe that she would one day attain great sanctity.

Whilst yet a child, feeling only distaste for the amusements natural to youth, she retired to secluded corners in the house, and recollected herself in prayer.

As a young girl, she avoided society, and it was her delight to pass much of her time in church and to prolong her prayers for several hours. At early age she consecrated herself to

God by a vow of virginity and began to mortify her body by fasts, the use of the discipline, and other austerities, desiring in this way to protect the flower of her purity. She was at all times a model of meekness and humility; for having lost her father, and her mother sinking under the weight of years and sickness, Margaret Mary was treated with such severity and harshness by those who were in authority in her home, that she was often in want of the necessaries of life. This state of things, as painful as it was unjust, lasted for several years; and was endured by her with the utmost patience; her consolation being to contemplate and imitate the sufferings of Jesus Christ.

At the age of nine she was admitted for the first time to receive the Most Holy Sacrament of the Eucharist; and this heavenly food enkindled in her heart an ardent love which was visible in her exterior.

Animated with a like charity for her neighbor, she grieved bitterly for the misery of so many children, who, neglected by their parents, were ignorant of the most essential truths of salvation, and were growing up in the practice of vice. For this reason she endeavored, with admirable patience, to instruct them on the mysteries of faith and to train them in virtue; and she constantly deprived herself of a good portion of her meals to feed these poor children.

Having fixed the choice of her heart on a Heavenly Spouse, she always refused the offers of marriage proposed to her, which would have been as honorable as advantageous; and in order to keep her word to her Divine Spouse, she thought of entering a cloister. After a long and serious consideration, and having sought to know the will of God in prayer, she went to a monastery of the Visitation of the Blessed Virgin Mary, in the city of Paray-le-Monial, in the diocese of Autun; she had then attained her twenty-third year.

Having conducted herself in the novitiate with a piety in keeping with the generous fervor and innocence of her past life, she was admitted to profession, and pronounced her solemn vows.

After her profession she advanced rapidly in the ways of perfection, and afforded to her sisters in religion a brilliant example of all virtues. She was distinguished by great humility, an extraordinary readiness to obey; an invariable patience in suffering, a perfect observance of the rule in every detail, an unremitting practice of bodily mortification and a constant love for prayer to which she gave herself day and night, and often was her soul disengaged from the senses and inundated with the dew of divine grace. When meditating on the sufferings of Christ, her soul was so deeply moved, and the fire of her love was so ardent, that for a considerable space of time she seemed to lose consciousness. Her remarkable virtues having excited the admiration of her companions, she was entrusted with the training of the novices; and a person more suitable for this office than the venerable Margaret Mary could not have been found, nor one more capable of encouraging by her example those who had entered on the path of perfection.

One day previous to her appointment to this office, when she was praying with great fervor before the Blessed Sacrament, Jesus Christ made known to her, that it was His desire to see established the worship of His Sacred Heart burning with love for mankind, and He committed to her this great work.

The venerable servant of God was astonished; her profound humility persuaded her that she was unworthy of so sublime a mission; nevertheless, in order to obey the commands she had received from Heaven, and to satisfy the desires she herself had of enkindling the fire of divine love in the hearts of men, she did all in her power, both with the religious of her monastery and with those over whom she had any influence, to spread the devotion, so that the Sacred Heart might receive from them all possible homage.

Blessed Margaret Mary had much to suffer in this undertaking, and met with innumerable obstacles. She was, however, never discouraged; but sustained by her confidence in the divine assistance, she labored with so much zeal and constancy, that with the help of God; and to the great profit of souls, the devotion spread and developed in the Church with wonderful rapidity.

Finally, desiring death as the means of being admitted to the heavenly nuptials, and wasted more by the flames of her love than by disease, she happily closed her life on earth the 16th of November, in the year 1690.

LITANY OF THE SACRED HEART

Lord, have mercy on us.
Jesus Christ, have mercy on us.
Lord, have mercy on us.
Jesus Christ, hear us.
Jesus Christ, graciously hear us.
God the Father of Heaven, *have mercy on us.*
God the Son, Redeemer of the world, *have mercy on us.*
God the Holy Ghost, *have mercy on us.*
Holy Trinity, one God, *have mercy on us.*
Heart of Jesus, *have mercy on us.*
Heart of Jesus, hypostatically united to the Eternal Word, *have mercy on us.*
Heart of Jesus, sanctuary of the Divinity, *have mercy on us.*
Heart of Jesus, tabernacle of the Most Holy Trinity, *have mercy on us.*
Heart of Jesus, temple of all sanctity, *have mercy on us.*
Heart of Jesus, fountain of all grace, *have mercy on us.*
Heart of Jesus, most meek, *have mercy on us.*
Heart of Jesus, most humble, *have mercy on us.*
Heart of Jesus, most obedient, *have mercy on us.*

Heart of Jesus, most chaste, *have mercy on us.*
Heart of Jesus, furnace of divine love, *have mercy on us.*
Heart of Jesus, source of contrition, *have mercy on us.*
Heart of Jesus, abyss of wisdom, *have mercy on us.*
Heart of Jesus, ocean of goodness, *have mercy on us.*
Heart of Jesus, throne of mercy, *have mercy on us.*
Heart of Jesus, model of all virtues, *have mercy on us.*
Heart of Jesus, sorrowful in the garden, *have mercy on us.*
Heart of Jesus, filled with reproaches, *have mercy on us.*
Heart of Jesus, broken for our sins, *have mercy on us.*
Heart of Jesus, made obedient even unto death, *have mercy on us.*
Heart of Jesus, pierced by a lance, *have mercy on us.* Heart of Jesus, refuge of sinners, *have mercy on us.*
Heart of Jesus, strength of the weak, *have mercy on us.*
Heart of Jesus, comfort of the afflicted, *have mercy on us.*
Heart of Jesus, support of the tempted, *have*

mercy on us.

Heart of Jesus, perseverance of the just, *have mercy on us.*

Heart of Jesus, hope of the dying, *have mercy on us.*

Heart of Jesus, joy of the blessed, *have mercy on us.*

Heart of Jesus, delight of all the saints, *have mercy on us.*

Lamb of God, who takest away the sins of the world, *spare us, O Jesus.*

Lamb of God, who takest away the sins of the world, g*raciously hear us, O Jesus.*

Lamb of God, who takest away the sins of the world, h*ave mercy on us, O Jesus.*

Jesus Christ, hear us.
Jesus Christ, graciously hear us.

℣. Jesus, meek and humble of Heart.
℟. Make our hearts like unto Thine.

PRAYER

Almighty and eternal God, cast Thine eyes on the Heart of Thy beloved Son; behold the satisfaction which He offers in the name of all sinners: listen to the praise which He gives to Thee for them; be appeased by His divine homage, and grant us mercy and the pardon of all our sins, in the name of Jesus Christ Thy son, who being God, livest and reignest with Thee in the unity of the Holy Ghost, forever and ever. Amen.

HYMN

Pity, my God, 'tis for our fatherland,
And for Thy Church we humbly bow in prayer;
Thy Vicar's captive, break his prison band;
Thy Church's losses in Thy might repair.
God of mighty power,
Take Thy Vicar's part;
Oh, save him in this hour
For Jesus' Sacred Heart.

Pity, my God, Thy Church in other lands,
The Swiss and German seek to break her walls;
Oh, may she keep, beneath the spoiler's hands,
Her faith to Thee, whatever else befalls.
God of mighty power,
Take Thy Vicar's part;
Oh, save him in this hour
For Jesus' Sacred Heart.

Pity, my God, on those misguided men
Who outrage Thee, but know not what they do;

In mercy wait, and draw them back again,
Their faith and love in sorrow to renew.
God of mighty power,
Take thy Vicar's part;
Oh, save him in this hour
For Jesus' Sacred Heart.

LITANY IN HONOR OF BLESSED MARGARET MARY

Lord, have mercy on us.
Jesus Christ, have mercy on us.
Lord, have mercy on us.
Jesus Christ, hear us.
Jesus Christ, graciously hear us.
God, the Father of Heaven. h*ave mercy on us.*
God the Son, Redeemer of the world, h*ave mercy on us.*
God the Holy Ghost, *have mercy on us.*
Holy Trinity, one God, *have mercy on us.*
Holy Mary, p*ray for us.*
Holy Mother of God, *pray for us.*
Holy Virgin of Virgins, *pray for us.*

St. John, *pray for us.*
St. Francis of Sales, *pray for us.*
St. Jane
 Frances, *pray for us.*
Blessed Margaret Mary, p*ray for us.*
Pearl of Great Price, p*ray for us.*
Flower of the Field, *pray for us.*
Lily of the Valley, *pray for us.*
Morning Rose, *pray for us.*
Child most dear to Mary, *pray for us.*
Incense of Sweet Odor, *pray for us.*
Palm of Patience, *pray for us.*
Treasure of Charity, *pray for us.*
Spouse most beloved of Christ, *pray for us.*
Violet of the garden of St. Francis of Sales, *pray for us.*
Star shining in the midst of clouds, *Pray for us.*
Rule of Obedience, *pray for us.*
Model of Mortification, *pray for us.*
Seraph before the Altar, *pray for us.*
*Sanc*tuary of the Heart of Jesus, *pray for us.*
Delight of the Heart of Jesus, *pray for us.*
Apostle of the Heart of Jesus, *pray for us.*
Plaintive Dove, *pray for us.*
Dove most Beautiful, *pray for us.*
Rock unmoved in the midst of tempests, p*ray for us.*
Mistress most gentle, *pray for us.*
Angel of Holy Counsel, p*ray for us.*

Terror of Demons, *pray for us.*
Merciful Intercessor for Sinners, *pray for us.*
Tender Solace of the Poor, *pray for us.*
Relief of the Sick, *pray for us.*
Holocaust of Divine Love, p*ray for us.*
New star of the Church, *pray for us.*
Joy of thy holy order, *pray for us.*
Glory of thy people, *pray for us.*
Lamb of God, who takest away the sins of the world, *spare us, O Lord.*
Lamb of God, who takest away the sins of the world, *graciously hear us, O Lord.*
Lamb of God, who takest away the sins of the world, *have mercy on us, O Lord.*
Jesus Christ, hear us.
Jesus Christ, graciously hear us.

PRAYER

O Lord Jesus Christ, who hast wonderfully revealed to the Blessed Margaret, Virgin, the unsearchable riches of Thy Heart, grant that we may by her merits, and following her example, may love Thee in all things and above all things, and may be found worthy to obtain an eternal resting-place in Thy Heart; Thou who being God, livest and reignest with God the Father, in the unity of the Holy Spirit, for ever and ever. Amen.

PRAYER TO BLESSED MARGARET MARY ALACOQUE

O Blessed Margaret Mary, thou whose sole desire was to see the Sacred Heart of thy divine Spouse known, adored, and loved, in Heaven and on earth, and who wast so deeply and so sadly grieved at the infidelities and ingratitude which It suffers from the greater part of mankind, obtain for us some share in the burning zeal which consumed thy heart, and the compassion which filled thy soul. May we, following thy example, make our lives a continual act of reparation for the outrages inflicted on the Sacred Heart of our divine Master. Amen.

Ingram Content Group UK Ltd.
Milton Keynes UK
UKHW011830060623
422972UK00002B/2

9 781957 066288